A SQUARE PEG

Conformity Isn't An Option

Gabriella Jaye

BALBOA.
PRESS

A DIVISION OF HAY HOUSE

Balboa Press books may be ordered through booksellers or by contacting:

Balboa Press
A Division of Hay House
1663 Liberty Drive
Bloomington, IN 47403
www.balboapress.com.au
1 (877) 407-4847

Because of the dynamic nature of the Internet, any web addresses or links contained in this book may have changed since publication and may no longer be valid. The views expressed in this work are solely those of the author and do not necessarily reflect the views of the publisher, and the publisher hereby disclaims any responsibility for them.

A Square Peg is a creative non-fiction memoir, with events and personalities depicted from the author's perspective, perceptions and memories. All names used in the narrative have been changed to protect individual identity. The author of this book does not dispense medical advice or prescribe the use of any technique as a form of treatment for physical or medical problems without the advice of a physician, either directly or indirectly. The intent of the author is only to offer information of a general nature to help you in your quest for understanding and wellbeing. In the event you use any of the information in this book for yourself, which is your constitutional right, the author and the publisher assume no responsibility for your actions.

Any people depicted in stock imagery provided by Thinkstock are models, and such images are being used for illustrative purposes only. Certain stock imagery © Thinkstock.

Print information available on the last page.

ISBN: 978-1-5043-1217-2 (sc)
ISBN: 978-1-5043-1218-9 (e)

Balboa Press rev. date: 01/30/2018

Square Peg in a Round Hole or **Round Peg in a Square Hole**… a misfit, especially a person unsuited for a position or activity. This idiom, with its graphic image of something that cannot fit, dates from the 19th century.

It is attributed to British philosopher and cleric Sydney Smith and is used to describe someone who doesn't fit in, isn't a team player.

PROLOGUE

Each day was filled with magic, with wonder, surprises and new adventures a constant companion and unexpected entertainment. Gabriella never knew what was going to happen next, all she knew and understood was that there was a never-ending supply of new things to see and do. Though young and tender in years she accepted the vastness of unanticipated and fascinating opportunities that were presented on a daily basis. Upon awakening each morning she felt excited about the possible thrilling and unusual new exploits that would unfold with surprising ease during the day.

Best of all she looked forward to recounting these experiences to the adults in her life. At the end of each day she eagerly anticipated her father's return. After the evening meal her parents relaxed and she commanded their undivided attention. It was with great delight that she shared the places she had seen and conversations held. The excitement bubbled over as she described in vivid detail the finest aspects of visions observed and deep conversations she had engaged in. With eyes sparkling and widely grinning mouth her exuberance was easy to observe.

From a very early age Gabriella exuded confidence and along with that an eagerness to learn and participate in all aspects of life as observed in the adult world around her. Questions raced out of her mouth with non-stop frequency. Often her exuberance was so strong that her speech became overly rapid, as words ran one into the other. Nothing dampened her spirit or enthusiasm.

There was nothing more exciting than the large family gatherings that took place regularly, and where birthdays, christenings and any other reason for sharing in the festivities of life provided an opportunity for the family clan to gather. Gabriella's eagerness and anticipation ran high. The gatherings presented an opportunity to share her escapades with even more people, who she confidently believed were as excited about them as she felt. She would wind her way around the large table and the many chairs, looking for a spare lap that she could climb up onto and where she could share her treasure trove of stories. Each time she shared her adventures she became more emboldened and animated. The adults in her life asked questions, listened intently and smiled indulgently.

There were other times, however, when her animation and exuberance became somewhat exhausting for the adults in her family. Comments such as, "Doesn't she ever stop talking?" or "Slow down a bit, you're talking too fast" were muttered occasionally. Gabriella was oblivious to the world of adults because she just knew that her world was much more exciting and interesting.

She was unaware her parents were concerned about her wellbeing, that they spent time discussing Gabriella's fascination with a world and reality that could not be seen. Family discussions ensued as Gabriella showed no sign of slowing down. Family activities to distract her attention failed to deter her from ongoing communication and journeys with invisible, or make-believe, friends.

Needless to say those adult conversations led to one conclusion and that was Gabriella needed to be tested or assessed in order to determine her mental state. Her parents feared that she might possibly have a mental illness or even be intellectually challenged. In those early days mental illness wasn't understood or socially accepted. All her parents were concerned about was whether Gabriella was normal or whether she would require special assistance. Her persistence in believing in make believe friends had tested their patience to the utmost degree, and they worried about her ability to cope with schooling, which was due to commence within the next couple of years.

Those concerns were rapidly allayed as it turned out that Gabriella's assessments found her to be highly intelligent, much to her parents' surprise and relief. This interaction with make believe friends had to be stopped and it wasn't long before a solution was found. Early entry into school was the outcome, and immediately Gabriella became entranced with this new experience. Her strong inquisitive drive to have adventures galore was fulfilled in the school environment. Each day provided new opportunities to talk, learn and to explore. It was a highly stimulating environment that provided ample distractions and rapidly gained her full attention. Gabriella loved talking, not because she loved the sound of her own voice but because she found life fascinating and was keen to share her observations and to ask countless questions. She may also have had somewhat of an extravert personality tendency, possibly something that might have been overlooked by her concerned family.

At about the same time a disturbing realization gradually dawned on Gabriella. Her family had humoured her when listening to the stories she shared and she began to sense their concern for her welfare. In fact, she became very aware of their disapproval and felt shattered within. What had been a precious thing to her now seemed to be tainted and unfitting. It was a sobering and sad day when that realization struck, finally settled in and took hold. In order to keep the adults in her life happy she had to say good-bye to her loving and beautiful invisible friends and to let go of the marvellous experiences and journeys. Regrettably, it was time to behave as was expected of her.

Sadly, with a heavy heart, Gabriella bade farewell to the friends who had enriched her life for so long. She understood, on a deep level, that she was letting go of her childhood and its inherent magic. Sadly her non-physical friends bade her farewell. It was time for Gabriella to focus on her human and everyday experiences and to become compliant with adult wishes and expectations. Gabriella's socialization into the human adult world was about to commence. The joys and innocence of childhood would rapidly become a distant memory.

"It's choice, not chance, that determines your destiny."

Jean Nidetch

CHAPTER 1

On the drive home I couldn't understand the feelings of unrest and being unsettled that seemed to plague me most days. There was nothing to be disturbed about. My life continued on as it had done for many years, with predictability and routine firmly established. Work was enjoyable and certainly provided plenty of variety, stimulation and challenges. My teaching career was mostly satisfying. It had nourished my soul and fed a constant desire to learn and grow, until recently anyway. But was it career that was the cause of the disturbing unrest? If not, then what could it be? I didn't really have the inclination to look too closely at my life, possibly due to an innate fear of what might be found if I delved too deeply.

Overall life was okay and at times even fulfilling. My marriage certainly wasn't made in heaven, but surely that wasn't unusual and wasn't sufficient reason to make any changes. Over the many years together I had adapted to the ups and downs of marriage, and if things weren't always ideal then there were ways to cope. The fact that I exercised compulsively was put down to a desire to maintain fitness; fully deluding myself that it was enjoyable and was beneficial to both health and wellbeing. It was impossible to recognize that my favourite daily workouts were a means of escaping from reality, along with the stresses inherent in that reality.

The reflections continued, albeit superficially, as I ran through a mental checklist of all the things that were good in life. Friends, especially, were important and over the years I had carved out and solidified some great friendships. The friendships were mixed, in terms of backgrounds and interests. Strong bonds had been forged through sport and fitness, as a shared passion for keeping healthy shaped those. Though social gatherings were held infrequently it was relaxing and exciting to chat about personal fitness and to be open to learning more about the mechanics and physiological aspects of health. Over the years a deep sense of camaraderie had evolved through these particular friendships.

I especially enjoyed my teaching friendship group, though that really didn't consist of many people despite the fact that I'd been teaching for quite a number of years. Similar ages, shared ideologies and a healthy sense of humour seemed to be the glue that sustained those particular friendships. If ever I was in trouble or needed urgent help these friends would be there to provide support just as I would be there in a reciprocal role if ever needed.

Then there were the shared friends, those Evan and I kept in touch with and occasionally spent enjoyable social time with. Being honest in this reflection, I finally acknowledged that in this particular group there was no one I felt I could trust with confidences, share my deepest secrets or feelings. But, of course there wasn't anything to share as life was going smoothly and everything looked pretty good. There was nothing to complain about despite the feelings of unrest that just wouldn't abate or leave. With that in mind I mentally continued down the list of friendships in an attempt to figure out a logical reason for this constant disturbing feeling of inner disquiet. Perhaps it lay within some aspect of relationships with others, I fleetingly thought.

Into mind popped family. Could they be considered friends or were they merely to be relegated to family status? Upon further reflection, though still not going too deep, I realized that there was no one in either my family or Evan's family that I felt particularly close to. Yet there were no disruptive elements tainting family relations. Amicable perhaps would be a better way to view them. Spending time with family actually felt more of an obligation or duty. Yes, if I were to be brutally honest that's how I viewed family, one where obligation seeped through all conversation and actions. Did that make me an evil or hard person? Or, was I perhaps lacking some gene that said you had to deeply love your birth family? If so, at that moment I certainly wasn't feeling the love. But this possibly could be attributed to the long and challenging history of family dynamics. That definitely was not something to reflect upon right at this moment as I continued the drive home.

What about the family I'd gained through marriage? It was a large family. There were cousins for my children to play with when younger and to mix with socially as they had grown older. There was a great deal of value in the children having that family stability and security. The adults were certainly a mixed bag and relations were always cordial. However, again being totally truthful, I admitted that I really felt different and couldn't see any common grounds for deep friendship. Holiday gatherings and small celebrations felt like a chore that had to be undertaken. Again there was that feeling of obligation, where it was important to put on a positive face and to conform. There was no dislike or animosity towards or between us. In a nutshell, I just didn't fit in despite the many years of interacting and socializing. There was little commonality, and there certainly wasn't anyone I could truly feel sufficiently comfortable with in order to open up about things that had happened or were really important or highly interesting.

Overall, there was a feeling of superficiality relating to family friendships, or so it appeared when viewed dispassionately. Yet I really didn't know or understand what could be done to change things. It seemed as though everyone in the family was playing a role and that each role was agreed upon unconsciously by the family collective. Maybe I was the only one feeling this way? Admittedly I'd never thought of it in this context before. Possibly this might just be something to reflect on more seriously at another time.

My mother had taught me well. Any time discussion arose around something that had happened previously my mother would say, "There's no point in talking about something you can't change". And that was that! Hearing statements like that time and again had had a powerful impact during my growing years and also throughout my adult life. Having adopted that particular mantra and attitude as my own I was feeling intensely uncomfortable with the inner disquiet this thought provoked. On a conscious level I couldn't fathom any valid reason for running through a checklist of friendships and reflecting on their relevance to my life or wellbeing. It really was a futile mind search, which certainly did nothing to alleviate the non-stop internal discomfort being experienced.

With my mind still meandering all over the place, another of my mother's constant sayings reverberated loudly into consciousness. "You're too sensitive" or expressed differently, "The trouble with you is that you're too sensitive". How many times had those words been uttered? For as long as I could remember I realized. Every time those words were uttered I had felt guilt and shame, as if it were a crime to actually feel things.

As an adult I could now chuckle inwardly at some of the things that had occurred when I was much younger. At the time though that sensitivity certainly had caused a lot of disharmony and upset within the family. Being naïve I had often had blurted out things while in adult company that probably would have been best left unspoken. On more than one occasion a guest in our home had made a statement about something obviously important to that individual and eager to be part of the conversation, I didn't hesitate to let all within earshot know that the person was telling a fib. The resultant outcome was massive embarrassment on my parents' part and a scolding received afterwards. Later, no matter how much I persisted in telling the truth of what I'd known, it didn't sit well to be called a liar by adults and to be told to only listen and to zip those loose lips!

Nearing home I mentally acknowledged that those earlier experiences ultimately stifled my ability to speak the truth clearly and honestly. I had learned to swallow or hold back my words due to those bitter experiences in the early formative years. Instead I had discovered the art of telling people what I intuitively knew they wanted to hear. It was certainly less stressful and there were fewer disruptions to family relations as a result. Despite this gradually acquired restraint my mother still found occasion over the years to remind me of my crime of being too sensitive. That criticism, unfortunately, also impacted the relationship with my mother in a rather negative way. I learned the hard way that open and honest communication about my feelings generally fell on deaf ears, so it was easier to say less and to hold the emotions within. At some point it was obvious that despite countless persistent attempts to create a loving bond of open communication with my mother that it would never happen. Emotions of anger surfaced unexpectedly from deep within as I understood the extent of what I'd missed out on. Realistically though there was no way of changing the dynamics of this particular relationship, and I felt sad that all previous attempts to forge a healthy relationship between us hadn't changed anything.

These were morose thoughts and there was no point in dwelling on what couldn't be changed. This prompted a quick veering of memories in a new direction. Next my thoughts dwelled on the forthcoming family holiday. Once a year we drove north to warmer weather, where we lazed, swam and walked on the beach for two weeks. Year after year this vacation had become something of a ritual, and while it was a lovely break after the chilly winter weather my thoughts involuntarily shifted in another direction. This was a memory I definitely wanted to stifle.

This particular memory wouldn't fade unfortunately. It was such a simple thing. A request made that was met with ridicule and a personal put down. It happened so quickly that at the time I hadn't had the gumption to question or challenge the comment. It was only later that I began to see this response was part of the bigger picture, that it was Evan's regular way of exerting control.

Professionally we both had busy teaching careers. In addition to the yearly sojourn to a more tropical climate, which necessitated many hours of driving, we also routinely made a shorter trip to another coastal area where we spent time with his family once or twice a year. On one such occasion as we were driving towards this destination I wistfully and unthinkingly made the suggestion that perhaps just for once it would be wonderful to spend a few days in the mountains, hiking trails, looking at waterfalls, enjoying different scenery and being among trees. Evan's response was quick and sharp, "What's wrong with you? Aren't you happy with what you've got?"

That specific suggestion was never raised again, but I had seethed inside for a long, long time. That particular trip soured any belief I held that marriage is meant to be a partnership and instead was merely something you just lived with because of the commitment that had been made all those years previously.

Now, however, my thoughts once again turned to the forthcoming vacation. I would be celebrating a major birthday milestone while away. For some reason turning forty felt like a biggie. Forty represented middle age, or that was my perception, and I wasn't especially thrilled about it nor was it something I was prepared for. Yet this year the birthday needed to be acknowledged differently. Admittedly birthdays in our family had been celebrated rather blandly over the years, with the only excitement about gaining another year saved for the children. This year would be different I vowed. It would be lovely to have a simple, yet classy piece of jewellery, something I owned little of and rarely wore. It was also time to go out to dinner and celebrate this significant milestone. It was time to put my foot down and insist that some things be done according to my wishes, for a change.

Pulling into the driveway I braced myself for what was to come next. Would the evening be pleasant and relaxing or would it be filled with tension? My hope was that it would be calming and comfortable as the day's work had been long and challenging. We had reached that point in our relationship where conversations revolved around the mundane. Sharing of feelings and incidents had become lackadaisical or practically non-existent. Mentally I acknowledged that the feelings of lack, of disquiet, were mine. The tension between us was there but was it my inner tension only, or was it more? I had no answers. All I could do was muddle through yet another day and hope for the best.

"The most important kind of freedom is to be what you really are. You trade in your reality for a role. You trade in your sense for an act. You give up your ability to feel, and in exchange, put on a mask. There can't be any large-scale revolution until there's a personal revolution, on an individual level. It's got to happen inside first."

Jim Morrison

CHAPTER 2

With some difficulty and a few frustrating challenges I managed to get my way. A lovely silver chain, just what I'd wanted, was my birthday present. Admittedly it had been my responsibility to guide Evan in the right direction, providing clear explanations as he seemed to have no idea of what would be suitable. It was sad that after all this time together he really didn't understand my likes or dislikes. The chain was simple yet elegant and it felt great to wear. The celebratory dinner was another story. Evan hadn't seemed overly enthusiastic by my insistence that it was important to celebrate my fortieth birthday. The fact that we rarely went out to dinner didn't bother him in the least. Nevertheless I was determined to enjoy a meal cooked by someone else. The venue, chosen by me was a small restaurant with funky décor and a varied, innovative menu. It certainly made for a change from the routine meals prepared at home.

Reasonably competent in the kitchen I had grown weary of the limited food choices consumed at home. Evan was a typical Australian, living on meat, chips and a few vegetables for dinner, night after night. Eight years earlier I'd changed to a vegetarian diet and loved the way my body felt due to eating foods that didn't sit heavy in the digestive system after each meal. Our children also were a tad leery of trying out the different meals I prepared, though not as reluctant as their father. Evening meal preparation wasn't my favourite chore. Food experimentation was a rarity in my kitchen. Hence a celebratory birthday was deeply important in more than one way. Regardless I listened to his grumbles and resistance to some of the menu items, attempting to coax him into broadening his range of food tolerances.

Sadly, I reflected nearly three years later, Evan hadn't changed. Nothing had changed in our lives. There was a whole world of experiences outside my existence that I was missing out on. Life surely had to be more than a mere repetition, day after day. At that stage the movie Groundhog Day hadn't yet been released. But that was my reality. I lived it with mind numbing monotony. Where was the laughter, the shared joy? Truthfully, I was close to breaking point. The restlessness had continued unabated. In fact, it had intensified. At the end of every day as the car neared home, about to turn the corner and head up the hill my stomach began to clench and tie up in knots; it felt as though it was being strangled. Exercising obsessively continued to be a way to combat the stress. "Guess it could be worse," I mused, "My de-stress prescription could have been chain smoking or enjoying a non-stop fling with alcohol."

Instinctively I knew that neither of those two options would help - an awareness I would be deeply grateful for in the years to come. Most days there was a litany of self-reminders that I was fortunate to be living this middle class existence. After all, we lived in a good neighbourhood, earned decent incomes, everyone was healthy. Yet, there was a distinct lack of friendship, communication or shared fun in the relationship. The distance felt arctic and seemed to grow further every year. Any suggestions for improving things were generally met with negative responses and put downs.

Seven years after we'd moved into our new home a dear friend and neighbour, Alison, commented, "It's taken him seven years to wear you down?"

"What do you mean?"

"When we first met you laughed a lot. You were enthusiastic, filled with life, and smiled all the time. You're not like that anymore. You've become quiet and don't say much. He's ground the life out of you."

I wasn't ready to hear those words then, but now they came back into mind with the force of a tornado. It really was time to find myself, and to make changes that would enable this to happen. And, obviously, to find the courage to carry those changes through irrespective of the outcomes.

Once that decision was made it felt as if an irresistible force went to work, carrying me to thoughts and actions never previously contemplated. It was impossible to any longer ignore the icky feelings within, knowing that I would end up sick or possibly even dying from an illness that could, even at this time, be festering within due to the ongoing inner stress and misery. Shifting focus I began to note the constancy of the put downs, the continuing nay-saying and the limited opportunities I had for expressing my real needs or perceptions. Self-observation was extremely illuminating. It was immediately evident that I was tight lipped when in company with friends. Any spontaneity was well and truly dead and buried. It was much easier to listen to people than to talk. As a conversationalist I would have been rated a fifteen out of ten for being super boring, and that was not how I remembered myself, or how I wanted to remain. Without realizing it I had gradually become incredibly dull and uninteresting, so boring that the thought of having a conversation with myself was unpalatable.

In no time at all I hesitantly confided my intentions to a friend. Anna, still single, provided a wealth of relevant information to assist in making changes. There were very few friends I confided in. Most were married and I instinctively felt they wouldn't like to hear about my marital woes, and about which there were deep seated feelings of guilt, shame and failure. Anna was grilled about the pros and cons of being single, what was to be expected should I choose to explore this option. Anna's sharing greatly reduced fears of the unknown. Simultaneously I took note of my finances, grateful for earning a reasonable income and so could afford to make changes. After a brief search an apartment was found not too far from the family home, in order to still be close to and provide for our youngest child. Slowly but steadily arrangements were made, mostly with great trepidation and anxiety.

"I'm leaving", I said, as boxes were being loaded into my car.

"What do you mean?" Evan said, standing still and looking as though in shock.

"I've done everything I can possibly do to make this marriage work. It's not working. It's impossible to talk. I can't do this any longer."

Feelings of intense anger, frustration, sadness and more engulfed me as I proceeded to move boxes, trip after trip. Our youngest child, still living at home was confused and asked questions. I refused to argue with Evan in front of our son, determined to maintain cordiality and respect for both.

"Why are you leaving?" my son asked.

Gently I asked, "Do you ever see your father and I hugging or kissing?" Inside I was crying, feeling incredible sadness for this precious child, and wondering how this separation would affect him.

"No," he replied, looking puzzled.

"It's normal for married people to hug or kiss. I'm sure you can't remember the last time you saw us doing either?"

"No, I can't."

"That's why I'm moving out. It's not normal for married people to live like your father and I do. We don't laugh or play together. We're like strangers sharing a house. I'm leaving because I don't ever want you to think that this is how a relationship is meant to be. A relationship can be so much more, and should be much more. And that's what you will learn in time."

Child custody sharing arrangements were worked out. I ached with emptiness knowing that it wasn't possible to have full time custody, but also knowing that my son needed the security of remaining in the family home. Evan ranted and kept telling me, "You're wrong" at every opportunity. Regardless of whatever I attempted to say those words were repeated *ad nauseum*. Finally, in desperation I suggested marriage counselling but that wasn't a welcome suggestion.

The next few months were tumultuous and often I floundered questioning my sanity in taking such a drastic step. Evan, feeling angry, puzzled and frustrated spent time sharing his version of events with my family, shared friends, family doctor and possibly anyone who would listen. His repetitive mantra was, "She's wrong". Upon hearing this I cringed, as this had been a familiar refrain during our years together. My parents provided no support or understanding, instead they raged and cried at my idiocy. It rapidly became obvious they felt the utmost sympathy and support for Evan. After one visit to the family doctor for a minor issue I quickly ditched that medical practice as both the doctor and his wife felt it their duty to counsel me on the lack of wisdom exhibited.

In taking such a drastic step I alienated practically everyone I'd ever known. I was the wicked woman, the one who had been radicalized by feminism, and more. Married friends obviously felt uncomfortable around me, my actions posed a perceived threat to the stability of their marriages. Even more disturbing was the fact that for some time when first single I was propositioned by numerous men I knew who were married and who had been considered as friends in my sporting circle. Having their services offered to scratch the sexual itch sickened me almost as much as the loss of practically all friendships. I felt totally isolated as the world I knew no longer existed. I'd been thrust into a new and greatly unfamiliar reality.

Despite Evan's non-stop entreaties to stop this madness I remained determined. Just the very thought of ever living in that same house was sufficient to turn my stomach. Possibly it was some instinctual knowing from within that I had to push forward that kept me resistant to his suggestions. On some deep level was the awareness that if I acceded to the non-stop pressures I would die within, that precious life spark would extinguish, though right then that life spark actually felt more dead than alive. Even to my rational mind that awareness seemed ludicrous, but it would not leave. Life had been set in a new direction, one that could not be deviated from, and one where direction or outcomes could not be seen or imagined.

Eventually Evan finally suggested marriage counselling. I agreed as it hopefully would put an end to his haranguing behaviour. There were no expectations around the marriage counselling session. In fact, there was only the one session in which I made it abundantly clear that there was no intention on my part to seek reconciliation. This decision was clearly expressed in simple and clear terms and was based upon my perceptions and experiences within the marriage in recent years. The fact that I was constantly 'wrong' had spurred me into moving into an environment where I would no longer feel uncertainty, guilt or shame. I knew that it was not healthy to risk going back into a situation where there might possibly be more of the same. A fragile determination to escape what I perceived to be emotional and mental disrespect strengthened my resolve. Despite assertions to the contrary that things would change I was not in the least bit convinced nor was I willing to risk it. I was done.

Still being unable to articulate or express myself as clearly as I liked it was time to seek help. At Anna's recommendation I found myself, for the first time ever, in a therapist's office. Under the guidance and gentle questioning my story poured out. Once started there was no stopping the flow of words. The therapist, from time to time, uttered the well-known questions, "How do you feel about this?" or "What was your feeling?"

Consistently my response began with, "I think I feel…"

To which the therapist countered with, "You think you feel? You're not feeling, you're thinking."

"I don't know what I feel. I can't feel."

"Yes, you can feel and you do feel. The issue is that you've suppressed your emotions for so long in order to survive an abusive situation, and it's easier to suppress them than it is to continually feel them. It's a natural self defence mechanism, one that's enabled you to function and appear normal to others."

Hearing this I was both stunned and puzzled as to how it would be possible to discover my real feelings. They certainly weren't evident. I considered myself to be a strong, rational person. Certainly didn't cry or complain so obviously was either impervious to emotions or possibly a stoic.

The therapist continued, "My dear, I'm more concerned about the emotional state of your husband and the welfare of your child. You are doing well, you've taken action to take care of yourself and you'll be fine."

With that she proceeded to prescribe activities that I could undertake in order to help tap into the suppressed emotions, with final words of warning and support given.

"Congratulations, you are about to embark upon a journey of self-exploration in order to truly know yourself. This is a journey, one that not many willingly undertake. You're brave and I see that you will succeed. I wish you all the best."

It was during this time, the first few months of living the single life that I felt completely lost and at sea. Being single in one's forties was frightening. Many years earlier I had left home and stepped right into marriage. Nothing had prepared me for the roller coaster ride life was about to unleash.

Luckily I had Anna who listened and provided practical insights and suggestions on how to survive being single in what I had rapidly come to view as foreign and alien territory. At the very beginning of this liberation from married life Anna was my muse and wise counsel. In the early days Anna listed a number of important things to be aware of. Among the list two edicts stood out, due largely to their unexpectedness. The first of these was to play the helpless female whenever needing help.

Anna, with the voice of experience, said, "Men love to help a female in distress. Ask for help when needed and always thank them profusely. It makes them feel good."

I wasn't sure about this, feeling that it sounded like manipulation but in time found that it was solid advice and could be applied to both males and females who provide assistance in any situation where it's needed. Showing gratitude or appreciation at that stage was unfamiliar but I was willing to give it a go.

Another piece of advice given by Anna totally stunned. Without drawing breath when going through her list of practicalities relevant to singledom Anna said, "Buy yourself a vibrator."

Shocked and with mouth agape my immediate response was, "Why?" No sooner was that single word uttered when meaning dawned. This was completely unexpected and certainly something that I'd never encountered previously. In fact, two words summed up my worldliness, or lack of it - naïve and unworldly. At this stage I wasn't sure if leaving the comfortable and routine boredom of marriage was worth the shock of being immersed in a new and unfamiliar world.

However, the biggest shock was still to come. Another friend, Lisa, dropped in for coffee and was extremely excited about an astrology reading she'd just had with a well known and popular astrologer. Lisa babbled on and on about it while my response was to tune out as it all seemed so inconsequential. Checking out weekly or monthly horoscopes in magazines was about as far as my interest or belief in the validity of astrology ranged. Astrology was for entertainment purposes only. Right?

Unexpectedly Lisa drew me back into the conversation saying, "This is real. She read me, told me things I'd never expected. Don't you believe it's possible?"

"Not really. It's probably just luck".

"You wouldn't be saying that if you had a session. In fact, I think that's just what you need. You can't judge something if you've not experienced it."

Those words were the equivalent to a dare. Dare to prove Lisa wrong and that rationally it's not possible to see someone's past, present or future just by looking as some astrological gobbledegook. No matter what I said Lisa kept going back to refuting any arguments put forward. With great reluctance I finally conceded, "Okay, how do I do it?"

At that time Jane's astrology readings were published in magazines so she must have been considered reliable and reputable, or so I assumed. Nevertheless that didn't diminish my scepticism or reluctance. But in keeping with the unspoken dare from Lisa there was no choice but to make an appointment, while mentally deriding myself for being foolish.

Some weeks later, sitting in Jane's comfortable office, my cynicism was clearly evident. Body language spoke volumes. I sat right back rigidly in the comfortable leather chair. Arms folded, legs crossed and a neutral, maybe even dismissive "You prove you're not a fake," expression on my face. Witnessing a scam was going to be interesting, I was sure she would waffle and be unable to pick up on any aspect of my life.

Wrong! By the end of the ninety minute astrology reading my body language had completely changed, I was leaning forward, hands cupping my face with arms resting on her desk. My mind was totally stunned by the accuracy of what she described. Personal things that had happened, a description of the significant events in life and more were described in vivid detail. There was information that no-one else could have known, which was now out in the open. Most interestingly, she effortlessly picked up on the recent marriage breakdown, said it was meant to be and then proceeded to describe what could be expected in the immediate future.

Loath for the session to end, I finally had the confirmation and reassurance needed. I was shifting gears, going in a new direction and that direction would provide both challenges and fulfilment. There would be no turning back. In fact, she strongly advised against reconsidering my actions saying that to do so would only result in further unhappiness and misery which would take many years to recover from. I walked out of her office, head held high with feelings of optimism for the first time in many years.

"Reality is purely a perception of the individual mind. It follows, that since no two minds are alike, no two perceptions of reality are alike. It further follows, that what reality is to one may seem complete madness to someone else."

Yefim Novikov

CHAPTER 3

It was an exciting, yet also fearful time of change on just about every level. I felt as though I'd stepped through the looking glass and landed in an unfamiliar and unimaginable landscape. Information seemed to catapult towards me with a rapidity never experienced before, and almost immediately I began to ravenously consume anything and everything that would help my personal growth. Having lived in an arid desert of routine for so long it was with relief that this lushness of knowledge and opportunities swarmed and enveloped me in new and exciting ways.

Teaching involved far more than going through the motions and dealing with the basics. Over the years countless workshops and seminars to upgrade skills and knowledge had been attended, some extremely valuable and others seemingly not so. One of these two day workshops in particular turned out to be especially helpful to my understanding of self. A lengthy questionnaire was completed prior to the two day workshop. The apparently non-related questions didn't seem to make sense nor was it possible to discern their purpose. It certainly didn't auger too well for the prospect of spending two long days sitting and concentrating.

Again my preconceptions were erroneous. The Myers Briggs Type Indicator, widely used in industry and private sectors, turned out to be fascinating and highly illuminating. The completed questionnaire had been analysed and I was able to identify and read about my personality type. It definitely made a great deal of sense and felt right. The workshop was geared to demonstrating how different personality types complement one another in the workplace. At one stage the facilitator asked me to come up to the whiteboard. There I was handed a coloured marker and told, "Follow my instructions and draw the shape I describe accordingly".

Everyone else in the room followed the instructions as they were read out one by one and were drawing their shapes on paper, while I cringed inwardly at being up front and on public display. My personality definitely was not one of those types that loved being the centre of attention, and yet here was the possibility of once again being told "Wrong".

At the end of the exercise the facilitator showed the group the shape pre-drawn on a sheet of paper. None of the many staff there had drawn a matching shape – except one person. I was surprised, even shocked, especially given that the instructions had sounded convoluted and definitely unrelated to anything familiar.

The facilitator explained, "This exercise is about intuition, how well your intuition responds to information as well as demonstrating your level of intuition in different situations." Turning to me she continued, "In all the years I've been administering the Myers Briggs Type Indicator I've never encountered anyone as intuitive as you. Your rating on the scale is the highest I've ever seen. It's literally off the charts as you can no doubt see on your analysis results."

Feelings of pleasure coursed through my body, though the feeling of being astonished also surfaced. It was hard to believe that I was intuitive, something that had never even crossed my mind. That fact possibly may have explained my frequent response when hearing someone else speaking about practically any subject. My common response often was, "I know". In fact, Evan had indicated great exasperation with my "I know" statement, which had been muttered frequently during our marriage. How in the world did I know? And often I wondered where that knowing had come from. Realistically though I saw myself as being more logical and rational, and could engage comfortably in all kinds of mental gymnastics with the best of them. This intuition ability brought about a whole new dimension to things and definitely needed further exploration.

From an early age all kinds of books had brought comfort, solace and provided a world of discovery and knowledge that had been avidly explored. After the revelations from this workshop a visit to a nearby bookstore resulted in a discovery of the self-help section, something I'd never known existed. No doubt about it, marriage had resulted in a numbed down mentality and it was time to change that. It was there in the bookstore that books on developing intuition were displayed in abundance and were savoured with great delight. While there a couple of books written by Jane Roberts, who channelled an entity called Seth were also purchased. These had been highly recommended by Anna. Overall I found the self-help section contained books previously not encountered in my reading history, yet there were many that beckoned invitingly into a new world of knowledge and potential.

Painfully and slowly the exercises set by the therapist were implemented and worked on as often as possible. These involved a great deal of writing as well as probing deep within, something that certainly had been avoided for too long. During this process there was a gradual increase in self-knowing and understanding developing. Surprisingly I actually discovered stubbornness and wilfulness, attributes I would never have seen in myself. With a changing mindset I was determined to follow through and be open to all possibilities in order to leave behind what now appeared to have previously been a narrow minded world view along with an extremely limiting existence. My reading range and interest shifted to incorporate books on spirituality, emotional healing, mysticism, channelling and just about everything that was called New Age.

Then unexpectedly disaster struck. Illness happened. Suddenly I was constantly tired, very pale and found it difficult to get through each day. In desperation an appointment was made to see a local doctor, one who didn't know my history but who was happy to have me on his patient list once I'd explained why it was impossible to continue seeing the previous family doctor. I had no intention of being on the receiving end of a repeat lecture on the folly of my actions in ending a long term marriage.

Blood tests confirmed mononucleosis, otherwise known as glandular fever or the 'kissing disease' as the doctor explained. That wasn't funny. Was I kissing anyone? Definitely not, that was the last thing on my mind. Rest was prescribed. When asked about dietary changes that could support recovery, the doctor said none were necessary as rest was the best medicine. That response wasn't satisfactory and a determination to learn more surfaced. His rest only prescription niggled and annoyed me. Guess that would have been my new best friend, intuition, kicking in strongly.

The next few months were an ordeal. It was painful to sit, stand, walk, or lie down. My poor body ached everywhere and constantly. It was difficult to read or watch television as the ability to concentrate had totally disappeared. The days were long, and being on three months' sick leave certainly wasn't an idyllic holiday, as all that was possible was rest! This was no picnic. Daily I chafed at the enforced painful confinement. In order to heal faster I did two things that ultimately proved to be highly beneficial for long term growth. Eventually I came to view the imposed time out from the world as a gift, though didn't necessarily understand it to be that way while it was happening.

A constant pain had taken up residence in my back; it was painful to move a muscle in any direction. Silent internal screams arose from deep within with every movement. I discovered that the human back has a lot of muscles. Move one and that in turn affects many other muscles. Breathing was relatively easy, movement had become agony. Thanks to Anna's recommendation an appointment was made with Sam, a massage therapist, which turned into weekly visits for some months. The appointments were a salve to my rigid and hard as a rock back. During the first visit I explained my situation and listed all the vitamins, herbs and other actions that were being taken to heal the body. "Is there anything else I could do to help my body recover?" I asked.

"No, but how did you know what you needed to do?" Sam responded.

"I read up on mononucleosis and what it does in the body and then figured it out. My doctor said that no dietary changes were needed but that didn't make sense."

My intuition was working and having received confirmation lifted the mood greatly. While having weekly massage on the tight as steel back I also admired and envied the therapist. He told me information about my life and the things that had been experienced, all of which were true. "How can you tell?" I quizzed.

"Your body is telling me."

"What do you mean?"

"Everything that happens in life is stored in your body; your emotions, stress, pain and more. I massage many people and every body tells a story, it's really a matter of tuning in to the body and learning its language."

Hearing that my interest was piqued, along with feelings of envy. This was possibly another piece of the puzzle to figure out. How to learn more about this? Where did I need to go to become a student of the human body? Surely it couldn't be too difficult. I'd always found learning came easy and had the belief that with motivation and application then anything was possible.

The second positive that eventuated from the enforced mononucleosis rest was subtle, yet powerful. During this time I eventually read as much as possible about the deeper meaning on life, devouring countless New Age books that initially spoke a different language to what I'd been used to previously. Yet with patience – after all I had so much time on my hands while resting – the language, concepts and meaning began to impact deeply. Previously not given to introspection there was now more than ample opportunity to engage in this previously unknown activity. This time out from the world offered a privileged opportunity to reflect on my life, its ups and downs, potential, wasted opportunities and more. Definitely a few home truths surfaced with clarity, and I knew that while a process of change and growth was happening that it was also time to prepare for changes within. I could no longer continue being who I'd been for so long, or who I'd pretended to be. The real challenge would be finding myself, as I didn't have a clue as to the identity of the real me.

Gradually energy returned, my body began to feel restored. Yet I wasn't the same. Perceptions and understanding had undergone a subtle change, though as yet only a shallow shift had taken place. Regaining strength and energy took longer. Focusing on doing the basics took priority. Evan and I settled into a routine of child care. In order to provide stability for our son a townhouse not too far from his father's place was purchased and life settled into something of a routine despite the ongoing inner changes taking place.

There were also the superficial and obvious changes, which in time I came to learn accompany major life changes. As the inner world, or landscape, changes the outer world in time ultimately reflects spiritual, emotional and mental growth. First sign of this change came with the purchase of a new car. The white family sedan was traded in for a compact red car. How I loved zipping around town in that powerful machine. Hairstyle was changed and coloured for the first time in my life. Ears were pierced and jewellery purchased and worn with gay abandon. Wardrobe changes followed. Most exciting and challenging of all the changes was leaving the stability of a teaching career and finding a whole new world of experiences in working for a government agency.

Concurrently the New Age exploration continued unabated and courses of study beckoned. Once I'd discovered the healing power of massage it wasn't long before I signed up for massage classes. It was fun practising my newly acquired skills on willing volunteers. In addition, there were countless coffees with colleagues and possible new friends where I would talk at length on topics about which my knowledge was limited but where I found myself spewing out a great deal of unfamiliar information. Time and again I would be asked, "Can you repeat that?"

"What part?"

After being provided with a response I'd have no option but to say, "I can't. I honestly don't remember what I said even though it made sense."

All too often annoyance was expressed at my inability to remember due to the fact that what had been shared was usually profoundly deep in meaning. It became frustrating, especially as thoughts of early onset dementia surfaced, resulting in further self-questioning and many doubts accompanying my credibility. These early expert ramblings on unfamiliar topics were the beginning of my channelling development.

On a logical and practical level it felt fantastic to be able to engage in New Age 'speak', as though I were a veteran. My understanding at times felt expansive and unlimited, especially when waffling on with lengthy explanations relating to the meaning of existence. All this was happening without having studied esteemed scholarly analyses on existentialism or any other esoteric teachings. All very heady stuff regardless of the fact that it fell into a field of study that I'd never considered undertaking.

A new world was opening up rapidly. Hunger for further knowledge and experience could only be appeased by digging more deeply. A number of friends began to express concern for my wellbeing, or maybe it was for my sanity? Well intentioned Christian colleagues offered kindly advice, saying that doing the devil's work (channelling or healing) could result in dire consequences. I wasn't convinced, so their warnings about the potential trouble I could find myself in fell on deaf ears. Was it a desire to learn more that drove my eagerness to explore all possibilities or was it intuition that was the guiding force? Or was it a case of ego resistance surfacing? No answer to this question was provided.

Of particular concern to my new found friends was the fact that I had begun hearing voices in my head. This had started slowly and gradually increased in intensity. I heard the voices clearly, often simple statements that made a lot of sense. Occasionally I asked questions about something and heard the answers expressed simply – all inside my head. Was this an indication of becoming delusional? Had I been taken over by entities? Was free will being taken over? These were some of the questions that were pondered frequently during quiet reflective moments. Any thoughts of possible schizophrenia were immediately discarded. Ego belief was strong that this could never be a possibility. There was no family history that I knew of anyway, of bi-polar, schizophrenia or any other mental health issue. In the meantime I continued asking questions and receiving answers in my head. The more this occurred the stronger and clearer the answers, which in time proved to be quite in depth.

"Spirituality is rebellion; religiousness is orthodoxy. Spirituality is individuality; religiousness is just remaining part of the crowd psychology. Religiousness keeps you a sheep, and spirituality is a lion's roar."

Osho - Ananta

CHAPTER 4

It was a whirlwind ride for a number of years. There was the exhilaration and enjoyment of new learning and opportunities combined with confrontations with the deepest of murkiest emotions, most of which had been suppressed from early childhood. The whole tumultuous time was really about attempting to find stability within in order to figure out the real me, the one that had been kept hidden and secret for over forty years. If I couldn't figure that out then I figured my future was going to be bleak. And I was determined, no matter what, to escape from the nightmarish mix of stunted, haunted and surreal emotions that had been buried deep but were now emerging without invitation.

Being thrust into the singles life was difficult, especially with the loss of the many friendships I'd known for most of my life. How was it possible to make genuine new friendships? Where could I meet like-minded people? I felt very alone and isolated for quite a long period of time, not sure just what would be the best possible way of navigating this new world reality. Ironically opportunities for meeting new people seemed to crop up regularly, though often it rapidly became apparent that there was little or no long term commonality in world views or beliefs. The feeling of connection that often exists when meeting someone new wasn't happening in most instances.

However, one such new friend luckily shared similar values and experiences and we rapidly spent time over coffees and lunches unburdening ourselves. Several times she mentioned Reiki, saying that it would be an ideal training for me. By this stage I'd already discovered the power of healing in my hands, including the ability to send healing over a distance so wasn't too interested in following up her recommendation. Fortunately for me she persisted and with great reluctance I signed up to complete the three day Reiki I course. Eventually I mentioned this course to another new friend and he indicated great interest in also doing the course. We decided it would be a positive thing to have a shared experience, and to have someone familiar to talk with about whatever transpired.

Days one and two of the Reiki training were extremely challenging. I observed others, felt there was little or no value in the exercises and generally was both unimpressed and disgruntled about investing time and money. Most of the participants had signed up to heal illness conditions. That certainly wasn't relevant in my case and I felt absolutely no connection with anyone or anything on the program. At the end of day two my friend and I went out for a quick evening meal after which he said, "Go home and rest. You look beat".

That night was sheer hell. There was no sleep, I tossed and turned, and felt as though I was being pummelled non-stop by spirit. Pain shot through my body constantly. There was no respite from the pounding, neither was any part of my body exempt from this thorough beating. Despite this there were no bruises on my body or any indication of the beating received, but I knew that what I'd felt all night long had been very real. The following morning I'd arranged to meet Jan, a friend from my teaching days, and go for an early brisk walk. With reluctance and dragging feet I met up with her.

"What the hell's happened to you?" she asked upon seeing me. "You look frightful, like a train wreck."

"I'll be okay, this will pass," came the familiar stoic response.

"Exactly what are you doing this weekend? If this is what it's doing to you I can't see that it's helping in any way."

Intuitively I knew that the ghostly, battered look wouldn't remain and by the end of our walk and talk was feeling much better. Jan also commented on that particular improvement before we parted, though she still expressed concern for my wellbeing. Upon arriving at the venue for the final day of Reiki I training my male friend took one look at me and asked, "What happened last night?"

"I got the shit beaten out of me. My ego received a pummelling the likes of which I never, ever want to get again!"

"Good. You needed to have it happen."

And with that comment the subject wasn't raised again. I found day three, the final day of Reiki training to be delightful and enjoyable. Had

I really been that egotistical? Obviously it was evident to others. Since that day I've remained deeply grateful for this massive wakeup call and have had many opportunities for remembering what it felt like.

How I loved doing the Reiki healing. My biggest fan and only client for a long time was myself. Daily I spent a minimum of thirty minutes in the evenings doing self-healing, while loving the feeling of peace and relaxation it induced in my body. The need to heal my emotional issues ran foremost in my mind. Was I obsessed? Possibly so, but that wasn't a deterrent. Working with, getting to know and understand the Reiki energy and feeling its impact became as important as continuing with the therapist's suggestions for finding my true and deeply buried feelings. The more digging deep that took place the more evident it became that my body was filled with what I came to refer to as "truckloads of suppressed emotions". These emotions had been shoved down deep and forgotten, hopefully never again to be revisited. Unfortunately the body doesn't forget, though the ego mind however loves compartmentalizing memories. My memories, long kept under lock and key, were just beginning to surface.

∞∞∞∞

My father was tall, with large feet and hands. Those hands were massive. As a young child it seemed my purpose in life was solely to annoy him, which happened often. Punishment for doing so meant having to pull down my pants, lean in an undignified manner over his legs as he seated himself comfortably on a chair. The punishment meted out always consisted of several painful smacks on my bare bottom. Eventually I figured out that the easiest way to avoid those excruciating smacks was to practice being invisible. By saying as little as possible there was less likelihood of aggravating him. Instinctively I also learned to survive by gauging his moods. Knowing when to retreat and when to speak required walking a fine line at times. In adulthood I came to understand that he was a tortured soul, one who was battling his own demons. Nevertheless those younger years often felt like agony as his moods were pervasive in the household. He spent many years seeking a reason for the meaning of life. In doing so he switched his religious affiliation with frequent regularity. It was not until he found the Catholic faith and became a convert that the tension at home increased tenfold.

He became a devout Catholic and that changed the household dynamics greatly. Laughter and enjoyment of life were severely impacted and restricted for many years. It felt as though the tone of what had been normal and acceptable changed overnight. As a young child I had no coping mechanisms nor was I able to fathom what was happening or why. My emotional response was to seethe internally due to feelings of loss along with a lack of understanding around the unexplained changes. My faith, what little there was, quickly died and could not be re-awakened. School friends found it difficult to believe that I didn't believe in God, saying that it was even more important to have faith during tough times. "Faith gets you through all things" I heard constantly. If God was about love and goodness then it definitely wasn't happening in my world and I wanted no part of it. By the age of thirteen God and I had parted ways, permanently, and to this day my perception and understanding of the God thing is greatly at odds with the teachings of the many religions and faith systems.

∞∞∞∞

No sooner had some sort of routine and regularity been established in my life than it once again destabilized with remarkable aplomb. My son, fed up with the routine of changing living quarters regularly due to shared custody arrangements informed me one Christmas Eve that he would be moving in with his father permanently. The divorce had impacted him badly. Teenage surliness was his constant mood, and for which I was unable to provide an antidote. It was challenging dealing with my emotional healing along with having to provide stability and support for his teenage mercurial tendencies. The blackest day of my life was the day after I'd been informed he would no longer be living with me on a regular basis. His words of appeasement about this change didn't feel real. It felt as if he was keen to move on, but wanted to do it diplomatically without hurting my feelings.

The years since finding my singledom hadn't been kind to him, turning him into an angry young man. No matter what I said or did it was never right. Accusatory looks and comments, negative responses and surliness had become the one constant in our communications. It was with heavy heart, knowing that I had no option but to acquiesce with his decision, which resulted in a painful acceptance of the situation. My son didn't like the person I was rapidly becoming. All he wanted was his old mother back, the one who baked and did all the things that regular mothers do. He didn't recognize this new mother and rebelled against it by being uncooperative and unresponsive.

Life in my home town became increasingly miserable and untenable. Work colleagues continued expressing their concern regarding the dangerous path my life was taking. A number of interventions were arranged in order to shift my involvement with spirituality and healing into conforming to socially acceptable behaviours. None were successful, though every time kindly advice was dispensed I felt even more alone and misunderstood. Perhaps my explanations were the problem. That possibility resulted in experimenting with different ways of sharing or communicating my understanding around spirituality and the nature of natural healing, but that didn't work initially. It felt as though everyone else was right and once again I was wrong. On reflection it became apparent that those individuals who expressed most concern for my wellbeing were deeply Christian in their beliefs. I must have been surrounded by well-meaning Christians whose purpose in life was to save those poor souls who were lost or doomed to hell. Obviously I was a walking around with a large bullseye on my body as I became a regular target for their well-intentioned preaching.

Realistically, the only way forward was to be agreeable with what other people expressed as the truth, even if it didn't feel right. Being part of a group meant conforming and wasn't that what I'd been doing all my life, pretending to be the same as everyone else?

Nevertheless, after listening to yet another religious explanation about the dangers of doing the devil's work I felt it was time to set the record straight. The objections to the healing work I was doing ranged from the sublime to the ridiculous. After all, according to the self-proclaimed experts, the only place that healing should take place was within the sanctuary of the church and under the auspices of the minister or priest, or so I was told repeatedly. Those comments were also accompanied by fears suggesting that I was engaged in dangerous practices. Horror of horrors, I could even be possessed by an evil entity that would take control of my thoughts and body.

Eventually after great deliberation an appropriate response was formulated, which was expressed every time I was approached about changing my ways. It went along these lines: "I practice living in peace, and doing no harm. My life is aligned with the Buddhist precepts of mindfulness and harmlessness. A significant portion of the world's population lives with a similar philosophy. If what I do is the devil's work then it is the same for many others worldwide." Once I'd formulated this response and asserted my rights to learning and practising energy healing (Reiki) the haranguing eased off, though the obvious scepticism of others remained evident.

As a consequence there was also a distinct cooling off with some of the potential new friendships that had been loosely formed, resulting in further feelings of alienation and aloneness. It seemed no matter the direction or opportunities taken that my life appeared destined to be one of constant rejection. My interest in the esoteric and unusual was not shared by most people. There was so much ancient knowledge and unexplainable phenomena that intrigued and fascinated. Life, as it appeared on the surface in the larger world, seemed superficial and lacking real depth.

At the same time the voices in my head continued speaking. Sometimes loudly, other times softly. It became comforting hearing the wisdom that was shared. Sometimes the wisdom was so profound that it almost felt earth shattering, at times bringing tears of joy to my eyes. How could I not have known this? How could I learn more? The desire to continue this journey of healing and understanding became stronger than anything else. Other times I temporarily questioned my mental stability. It wasn't normal to hear voices and it certainly wasn't normal to give them credibility. Mental health issues weren't discussed publicly then. Due to the fact that I had frequently been told that I was wrong it definitely wasn't in my best interests to advertise the fact that I regularly heard voices in my head.

Then realization finally dawned. It was one of those exciting light bulb moments. As a young child I'd heard the voices and had had fantastic conversations with them. The voices had returned upon the ending of my marriage. They were familiar and had come in loud and clear. They felt like long lost family. This was the reason they presented no stress or threat to my wellbeing. They were family! With this realization dawning, the joy of reuniting with them was bitter sweet. I'd missed them greatly for nearly forty years, yet actually hadn't realized they had even disappeared out of my life. It was only with the reconnection occurring that the loss of their companionship for many years was felt. It was apparent that the ending of my marriage signified a turning point in life. It was also evident that I was on a steep learning curve, one that was only just beginning.

It was with reluctance that I applied for a job transfer out of the city to a smaller, distant town. Relations with my son continued to deteriorate to the point where I knew that staying would further exacerbate our fragile relationship. A three month transfer might just provide some breathing space, and hopefully would allow us to appreciate and understand one another better. A change of scenery from well-meaning Christians might also be beneficial. I was weary of having to explain myself, my life or beliefs. Little did I know that the transfer would be the real beginning of what ended up being an incredible journey, one that took me further than could ever have been anticipated. There would be no returning back to the start or even to where I'd left off. I was about to embark upon a magical carpet ride, though of course it didn't feel that way most of the time.

"To let go is to fear less and love more."

Unknown

CHAPTER 5

It continued to be a new vista. Unfamiliar and uncertain terrain confronted me at every turn. Being married for nearly a quarter of a century had not provided the qualifications or experience to deal with anything out of the ordinary. Living a safe, comfortable and routine lifestyle prevented the opportunity for gradual acclimatization into new territories or opportunities. I had lived in the one city for most of my life, travelled only to a few places with family. My world had been narrow and definitely limiting. The skills needed for adaptability and coping with change were imposed rapidly once I'd stepped out of the old paradigm. Overall it felt like undertaking a journey with no maps or navigation aids. Flying by the seat of my pants, which was to become the norm, was daunting and at times even frightening. This was how I learned to find inner courage and overcome fears. The next few years involved trial by fire, testing of strength and self-belief of a level I'd never thought possible.

Despite the travails of emotional healing and the pain of finding myself there were also moments of sheer joy and exhilaration. That yearned for vacation in the mountains was one of my first forays into a new life. Five days spent hiking trails and abseiling down sheer cliffs fuelled an incredibly strong desire to explore further options for getting up close and intimate with Mother Nature. I felt her calling. The healing calmness I found when outside, whether taking a stroll or hiking for days on end was a soothing salve to a wounded soul. Every avenue for experiencing yet another outdoor thrill was happily explored. One adventure after the other was eagerly sought and tried. The new adventures resulted in increased self-confidence, along with considerable skill building. Best of all, the element of shared fun and laughter with like-minded adventurous people was a much needed balm to a sore and bruised soul.

"I don't understand why you're doing all this. I certainly have never done anything like what you're doing" my elderly father asked. His tone and stance demonstrated clearly that he thought I'd lost a few marbles. After all, how many people in their mid-forties suddenly actively engaged in exploring caves, enjoyed hot air ballooning, spent weekends kayaking, took up cross-country skiing and spent days hiking trails in different states? This new me was totally unrecognizable to my parents and puzzled them greatly.

"That's because I have no intention of reaching your age and wishing I'd lived life to the fullest instead of playing it safe. It's my aim to have no regrets about opportunities that weren't taken. There is so much more to see and do in the world and I intend making the most of every chance that's presented," I responded.

The roller coaster of emotions, the pain of feeling isolated faded into nothingness when out and about exploring the world. The adrenaline charge from fresh air, exercise, travel to foreign places and more, amply balanced out a life that otherwise would have been unbearable. It was nature, in all its majestic splendour and its healing energies that righted erratic moods and kept the real possibility of depression at bay.

The strong desire to push forward and explore further was fuelled by a book that just happened to find its way into my hands shortly after the marriage ended. This particular book, *Feel the Fear and do it Anyway* by Susan Jeffers provided the blueprint for both learning more about those inner demons and for conquering them. I used the book as a reference guide, delving deeper and deeper into the countless fears contained within this particular and unfamiliar psyche. Interestingly my initial focus was on overcoming a terrifying fear of heights. Applying the suggested strategies to desensitize those fears was tough, but eventually there was massive improvement. The true gift, however, was that the more I used the book as a reference source and applied the various suggested strategies the more that sub-conscious fears emerged from within.

It was a lengthy process, time consuming and challenging. Yet in the five years before the job transfer occurred I had already overcome countless inner fears that I'd not known even existed. Did this mean that there was no further inner work required? Obviously I thought so, and again it didn't take long to realize that basically I'd only graduated from prep school. The serious learning challenges were about to commence. Despite previously being hammered by spirit, or non-physical beings during Reiki I training, there was obviously still some evidence of ego's strong existence within. More opportunities for living from the heart instead of the mind were gearing up to present further challenges.

Arrangements made. Airline ticket booked. Excitement within bubbled up. This was definitely going to be an exciting time. My unbridled optimism chose to ignore the words of caution that had been solemnly shared by work colleagues. This was my big adventure. Three months on work transfer to a totally unfamiliar environment might present some challenges or adjustment but surely after everything that had happened in the previous five years nothing else could be more daunting. This would be a cinch. My greatest sadness was in leaving my youngest son for so long, but promises about keeping in touch buoyed my spirits.

Reality struck shortly after. Maybe optimism had totally screwed up or that highly developed intuition had gone on leave without notifying me! Upon arrival in a small remote Australian town it rapidly became evident that this was nothing as expected. A mental adjustment needed to be made immediately. This was not a simple thing to do as the town and its inhabitants seemed to be living in a different era. All the luxuries taken for granted in a city were missing. Both climate and landscape were harsh and unforgiving. Slowly I adjusted to the different pace, lifestyle and attitudes. Everything seemed to move more slowly and things were never as straightforward as the bureaucracy I'd become accustomed to.

If I'd been hoping to find a community of like-minded souls then that was initially another disappointment. The basics of survival seemed to be of foremost necessity. In retrospect, nowadays I'd have to say that the people were predominantly of redneck, or bogan, tendencies. Yet I came to love it all, came to appreciate and understand all that was encompassed in living in isolation away from the bright city lights. The experience actually reflected, on another level, the feelings of isolation I'd experienced most of my life. It was time to grow up, to grow spiritual muscle and to begin to fully understand the nature of what being spirit in a human body really meant.

The job entailed travelling vast distances, being accountable for government monies being spent and attending countless meetings. It was typical bureaucracy yet the difference here was that I was seeing the process at the grass roots level, very different to processing papers in the distant bureaucratic ivory towers situated in the city. The regular work travel often entailed overnight stays in hotel rooms that had seen better days. These accommodation experiences came to be dreaded, and even feared. Nevertheless, it had all started innocuously. After a day's travel and meetings, followed by a quick evening meal I looked forward to a decent night's sleep before the next day's meetings. Unfortunately that decent sleep didn't happen after the first few trips on the road. Nightmares of epic proportion seeped in, resulting in intense fear. This happened regularly, once started, regardless of the hotel's location or accommodation quality. In the nightmares I was plagued, chased and confronted by black demon beings, determined to get to me and to gain possession. The realism of each nightmare was sufficient to awaken me, soaked in perspiration with fear oozing out of every skin pore. There seemed to be no end to these nightmares. Of course there was no sharing of these demonic experiences, as it was certainly not my wish to be scorned or derided by colleagues.

All the strategies I'd read about for overcoming fears hadn't covered fears experienced during sleep time, not as far as I could recall at that stage anyway. This was an entirely new proposition. It was obvious that using the suggested strategies from the book in a logical and purposeful way during waking hours really wouldn't work during sleep. I was stumped. That didn't stop the mind from attempting to grapple with this new challenge. On some deep, possibly intuitive, level I knew it was possible to be freed from the intense nightmare fears.

As a young child I'd sometimes had nightmares and woken up screaming and shaking. Those nightmares were always about being bitten by a poisonous spider, and upon being woken up from the fright would swear that I'd actually felt the spider bite. My parents would switch the light on and would search for the bite marks on my body, never finding any. Ironically throughout life I'd also had a recurring dream about walking through massive viper nests. These were not nightmares. I always felt completely safe, even comfortable being surrounded by and with snakes and was never bitten in any of that particular recurring dream.

This was different. These demonic figures were attempting to take possession of my soul. I felt it at a deep level. Thus began the practice of saying mantras to keep me safe during sleep. Prayer was not an option. God and I had parted ways many years earlier. Instead I'd come to the realization that the power lay within, and was not from an external source. Alas, the mantras were insufficient protection. However, due to going within to resolve the problem there actually was a straight forward solution, which became evident not long after all the inner reflection and exploration for a way out of the dilemma.

The next time the nightmare happened it began as it always began. In the nightmare I was in my particular space or room and the demons came in. There was always more than one. They were large, deep black and menacing as they approached. Normally in the dream I would scream, run frantically and would be chased and it was at this point that I always woke up. This time however I stood my ground and faced them. The anger within was intense and fiery. The feeling of being violated was even stronger. "How dare you! Who the hell do you think you are? Get the fuck out of my space and never return," I shouted with strength and clarity in my voice. They went and never returned.

It was that simple. I was dumbstruck. To think that I'd actually taken conscious control in a dream or nightmare state was a completely new experience. Talk about baptism by fire! From that point in time it was possible to take conscious control or intervention during dreams. It wasn't needed often, yet when it occurred it always felt right. Possibly this was the voice of my soul asserting itself, being clear about boundaries. My ego mind was in awe about this turn in events despite the fact that there was no one to share the experience with. How I would have loved to find just one friend in this small remote town. That yearning didn't in any way diminish the learning and understanding that had occurred. This time away was definitely one of developing spiritual strength and emotional muscle. I consoled myself by reflecting on the fact that there are times in life when journeys need to be undertaken in a solitary manner.

No sooner had I come to this understanding and acceptance than things actually changed. It all started from a brief innocuous encounter in the local supermarket. Cordial words were exchanged. It was a general conversation about some inane topic that led to a suggestion that we meet up for a coffee later in the week. From that point on life in this small town isolated by distance became interesting. Suddenly I found a like-minded community, a place where I felt totally at home. These were individuals who sought deeper meaning in life, who questioned the *status quo* and who were marching to the beat of their own particular drum. Possibly these individuals would have been labelled misfits by the mainstream population. That didn't matter. I'd grown up during the sixties and seventies and witnessed the seeds of global change that had emerged and been then suppressed. On a deeper level I felt a kinship with rebellious spirits; their unacceptance and questioning of the *status quo* frequently resonated strongly.

In no time at all I became involved in further learning. Spiritual healing, channelling sessions, meditation groups, psychic fairs, past lives, crystals, soul retrieval and more became the norm in my life. It was fascinating being immersed in this new but yet familiar culture. What was even more intriguing was a strong desire to delve further into what motivated individuals. It's often easy to skate on the surface when learning or experiencing new things. My interest was in examining concepts and topics more deeply in order to understand what was innate in an individual as compared with what had been learned through experience. My questioning, via intuition, often took me into other lifetimes that an individual had lived. Those experiences and memories from other lifetimes often remained and were carried into the present life, and would present challenges for the particular individuals. It was as though I could scan a person's energy body and read what was contained within from different lifetimes.

I'm definitely not a Karl Jung or Sigmund Freud, or even trained in psychology. Yet it felt as though I understood with absolute conviction and precision what was going on within an individual's psyche. It was effortless, interesting and a tad intimidating at times. Here I will admit to having Romany Gypsy blood somewhere in my lineage so possibly that may contribute to my abilities. Psychic gifts also run through the family generations. It was with this particular group of like-minded souls that it was possible to feel fully comfortable with my abilities, such as they were. There was no need to explain or justify. Most importantly there were no feelings of shame or guilt for being different or for not fitting in with the general worldview of what being normal is. Needless to say my office colleagues had no idea. I lived two distinctly different lives while on transfer and it wasn't in the least bit bothersome.

One night, woken from a deep sleep I saw green and red lights flashing outside. The house I was staying in was situated between two streets. A regular street out the front and behind the backyard there was a fence and beyond that another road. The flashing lights seemed to be coming from the road out the back. Normally police lights are red and blue but these were unambiguously red and green. Definitely very puzzling but being curious I got out of bed, walked out of the house and headed towards the back, wearing only nightwear. That's the last thing I remember until sometime later when I found myself standing on the paved path near the back door. There was liquid seeping from my vagina, running down my legs. I felt incredibly calm and collected, went back to bed and straight to sleep.

The following morning my mind went into overdrive. My intuitive knowing was that I'd been abducted, boarded an alien space craft and had had my eggs harvested. Given my countless interactions with non-physical beings from a very early age this wasn't implausible. When reading about other people's accounts of alien abductions years later the red and green lights were mentioned in countless stories. This experience was not my only contact with alien space craft, but it was the first incident where I'd had some distinct recall. Surprisingly there had been no fear at the time or afterwards, and that was an unusual response as most abductees retained horror fear memories and stories.

During meditations I was blessed to be connected with Aboriginal spirits. One in particular stayed with me for many months. Clairvoyantly I saw him clearly. He would stand erect on one leg with the other bent at the knee resting on the knee of the straight leg. It seemed to be his particular and preferred pose, and in one hand he would be holding a long spear. His build was slight and very slim. The only clothing he wore was a small scrap of material covering his lower torso. His hair was unruly, definitely unwashed and his body covered with dust. He was from the desert and came from the Dreaming Time, so he told me. During meditation and even during sleep he came and taught me Aboriginal culture, showed me sacred places and explained their meaning. In one such meditation we were roaming over what appeared to be desolate outback country and he pointed to a particular area in the distance containing rocks and sparse vegetation and said, "Men's sacred place".

"Will you show me?" I asked.

"Men's business. You are woman, not for you," came the brief response.

Darn! My curiosity evidently wasn't going to be satisfied on this particular occasion. At other times I heard his clap sticks, which were his way of getting my attention. When he spoke I listened intently. The wisdom and knowledge shared continued for some months and was always expressed simply and with reverence.

When it was time for the job transfer to end, not after three months as intended but ten months instead, I left feeling deeply enriched knowing that this time away was a hiatus, a step made in the right direction. My next step would further cement my life in this new direction. I would not be returning to the city that I'd left. There could be no going back.

"The greater danger for most of us lies not in setting our aim too high and falling short, but in setting our aim too low and achieving our mark."

Michaelangelo

CHAPTER 6

A significant highlight of my time in the outback was totally unexpected, yet enthralling, and the memory lingers to this day. My relatively newly acquired habit of exploring nature was carried out extensively, even in this harsh environment. No matter where I drove or walked there was expansive Mother Nature in her elemental best. Water holes, gorges and unusual rock formations were explored. It was as if this wild and ancient land shared its stories everywhere I went.

The night sky was clear and starry. A mixed group of strangers had come together to explore ravines, gorges and rocky outcrops one weekend. Accommodation on that particular night was on a plateau covered with spinifex grasses and termite mounds. A fire glowed for hours and we sat, relaxed and enjoyed conversation, reliving the day's strenuous explorations and discoveries. For the first time ever I slept under the skies. Lying in my sleeping bag, on the firm ground, all that was visible to the naked eye were zillions of bright, twinkling stars. The longer I lay there mesmerized by the sheer magnitude and magnificence of the night sky the closer the stars seemed to be. It felt as though all I had to do was reach up with my hands and I'd touch them. A feeling of ineffable peace suffused my body. I was as one with all of creation.

Memories from earlier days surfaced. As a child I'd been fascinated by the stars, and every opportunity to gaze intently at the night sky was seized. Books were studied in order to learn about the constellations and how to identify them. With longing so deep I yearned to be out there in the distant cosmos. A feeling so instinctual told me that this was where my home was, that I didn't belong on Earth. The memory of those feelings surfaced, along with another more recent memory. This later event had occurred just prior to leaving the city and heading into this remote territory. I'd scheduled a massage with another therapist, someone I'd only recently met. During the session I received a scolding. It certainly felt like a scolding but was obviously a message that needed to be heard.

"It's time to let go of the yearning to go home. You've chosen to be on this planet at this particular time. You have work to do. You are not meant to go home now. Accept this fact and get on with your life."

As I lay under the starlit sky I reflected on those words and acknowledged the rightness of them. That, however, still didn't take away the yearning that would not abate. I finally acknowledged that despite the deep love I felt for the planet Earth was not home and never would be. Possibly this might also be the reason I felt extremely comfortable hearing the voices in my head. They were reminiscent of a home that I knew existed but couldn't yet fathom or understand in my mind.

The following morning I awoke feeling completely refreshed after one of the best night's sleep ever. It only occurred to me several days later that not once had there been any concern about the possibility of having scary encounters during the night with any wildlife in the area. Venomous snakes, spiders or scorpions could easily have made their way into our campsite, and could easily have nestled up close and personal with any one of the group.

It was with mixed emotions that I left the small town and its isolation behind. The ten months there had been well spent. While I no longer felt as different from or unaccepted by others I was still grappling with finding myself and my place in this world. My next destination was another city, this one with a vibe that was totally different to the one that I'd left behind ten months earlier.

Bureaucracy is rigid, highly structured and certainly by this stage in my life wasn't a good match with my new found interests. However, after extensive interviews I'd successfully gained a position in another city within the same organization. Consciously it was my intention to broaden my skills base along with applying the extensive knowledge of all that had been experienced previously within the organization. Unfortunately the management and staff of this particular office were irate that an outsider had been selected for the vacant position. From the first day in the office I was treated like a pariah; my presence there was not welcomed. This presented a dilemma. Basic needs such as earning income to pay for accommodation, food and living costs still had to be met. Yet remaining in an intensely hostile work environment certainly was not conducive to mental or emotional health.

An alternative solution was needed, and sooner rather than later. From almost the very beginning a plan of escape began formulating. The words of wisdom shared years earlier by the astrologer kept whizzing around my mind. "When it seems that every door of opportunity closes just as you are about to walk through it, it is not an indication of failure or wrong doing on your part. It's the universe gently guiding you to where you're meant to be."

From my perspective the problem was that too many doors of opportunity had been closing in recent years. Every endeavour to move up the career ladder in both education and the bureaucracy had fizzled with remarkable speed, irrespective of study, intention and application. There had never been any indication of poor work ethics or performance on my part, in fact my work output and results had been amply demonstrated and often commended. It suddenly became blindingly obvious that this particular direction of focus wasn't meant to be. Climbing the career ladder within the bureaucracy was looking as unlikely as climbing Mt Everest at this stage. This conclusion led to the fearful and challenging prospect of making a radical career change, one where I was no longer an employee but instead took on the responsibility of self-employment, a terrifying prospect never previously entertained. Thoughts of death or self-destruction were preferable options at this point in time, though not really feasible.

Mentally I gave myself twelve months in which to create a vague, as yet unformulated self-employment career opportunity. An inspiring statement by Patrick Overton became my daily mantra, and repeated as a means of shoring up mental and emotional courage.

"When you come to the edge of all the light you have, and must take a step into the darkness of the unknown, believe that one of two things will happen to you: either there will be something solid for you to stand on, or, you will be taught to fly."

This simple yet profound quote helped maintain my sanity in the search for direction and purpose. This particular statement, printed on paper, was stuck on the fridge door and each day was read and reaffirmed with precision and dedication. Slowly I set up a healing practice, doing massage and Reiki, initially offering free sessions to anyone willing to accept my generosity and to also provide feedback.

This was to build up confidence along with providing an indication as to whether or not a natural therapies practice would provide the financial income needed for survival.

Courses of further training were taken advantage of on weekends. Most were in the natural therapies field while simultaneously regular intensive research on self-employment skills, legal and tax requirements and more were also studied. The day job in the bureaucracy was a waste of time as management basically provided little or no work, continuing to demonstrate their displeasure that an outsider had taken up residence in their domain. This continued despite my persistence in attempting to seek gainful productivity during office hours. Eventually the lack of meaningful employment there provided ample time at work for personal reading and research.

Feelings of not fitting in, of not being accepted or the need to conform no longer consumed my awareness. They were still there and the office environment only heightened the differences in countless ways. Instead of feeling weakened and inadequate within there was determination to find a niche, or place where comfort and acceptance were the norm. Instinctively the awareness surfaced that in order to be accepted I had to accept myself. This was definitely easier said than done given that for most of my life I'd been all too aware of, and felt, my unacceptable differences.

∞∞∞∞

Teenage years are never easy. Peer pressure is intense and constant. The sense of self is still forming. Identity is greatly tied to what is held to be the acceptable norm. I took my cues for behaviour and speech from what others said and did. The pretence of enjoyment and participation in activities wasn't always convincing, despite my best efforts. Yet taking part in the teenage rituals of smoking a cigarette or drinking alcohol was a rite of passage. I watched others drink to excess, to party like there was no tomorrow and to find joy in riding aimlessly around town looking for kicks and could only pretend to be of like mind and interest. Radio, music and magazines determined what to wear and how to behave. It all felt foreign and most times I saw myself as the outsider looking through a window while others seemed to really enjoy whatever was happening. Going through the motions seemed the safest and most acceptable thing to do.

What was the point of it all? Was there any meaning or purpose to it? These and other questions plagued me constantly. I only knew that there was no other option. Be like everyone else. Espouse similar values, attitudes and beliefs. Everything would work out okay in the end when adopting the shared core values along with a similar lifestyle. Above all don't question too closely, especially when it makes others uncomfortable. My enculturation was complete. By the late teens I'd been indoctrinated into believing the myths perpetuated through the generations. Get a job. Get married. Have children. Oh, and let's not forget the part about living happily ever after!

My one single outstanding and unforgettable moment of rebellion during this time felt exhilarating. School wasn't inspiring and I'd figured that the big, wide world would be far more interesting. Becoming a high school dropout wasn't a big deal despite the disastrous outcomes predicted by parents and teachers alike. I'd learned to play the game throughout school. Academic results were above average but any hopes of following my heart's desire of becoming a physiotherapist had been totally dashed so there really wasn't any point in staying at school. At that time tertiary education costs were high; my parents couldn't afford to send me to university. Debilitating college loans weren't even a fact of life in those Neanderthal days.

Instead it didn't take long to discover that life outside school involved both tedium and repetition. Simultaneously though there was a greater sense of freedom and enjoyment of new experiences still to be explored. It wasn't until I was married and Evan decided that teaching would be a good career for me that once again the rebel within was squashed. His reasoning was that teaching involved shorter working hours and longer holidays and would be the perfect job for his wife and mother of his children. That meant going back to the studies, getting qualifications and once again playing the game. This time I went into it with my eyes wide open realizing that teaching would provide a decent income and offer a lifestyle of that would be suitable.

Moments of restlessness and dissatisfaction would surface throughout the years, and were quickly denied. I had it all. Marriage, children and career. The only thing missing was the happily ever after.

However, obviously the fault for feeling restless and dissatisfied rested solely on my shoulders. I really had nothing to complain about in terms of material comfort. When younger my father's constant refrain whenever I didn't like a certain food or something else was always, "Be grateful. Think of all the starving children in Africa", or some other similar refrain. My fault. My wrong. Always.

∞∞∞∞

The office job in the city lasted just over twelve months. Time and energy were spent assiduously and rigorously preparing for self-employment. To this end it was glaringly obvious that my self-esteem and perception required a massive overhaul. Did I like myself? No. Did I have enough confidence? No. Regardless of these shortcomings there was plenty of bravado within but I quickly realized this would only suffice until the first serious challenges arose. A multi-pronged approach was adopted. The practicalities of study, learning and establishing a small business were easily handled. What was more difficult was preparing the inside, the inner self, the voice of doubt and uncertainty around my abilities to survive financially, mentally and emotionally. To this end mantras, along with self-inflicted mental butt kicking were put to excessive use.

The daily bus trip to and from the office provided an excellent opportunity for inner work. During the thirty minute trip each way constant repetition of mantras were running through my mind, all affirming self-love, acceptance, capability and more. Repetition and more repetition, statements such as, "I love myself. I am lovable. I love life. I am successful. I am confident," were mentally muttered continually. Every thirty minute trip seemed endless. However I was determined to learn and acquire a new found status of self-love. No more self-deprecations or self-abuse. Intuitively I knew my treatment of myself needed an overhaul and was long overdue. Instead flowers were purchased at least once a week for my personal enjoyment. I began to feel good about treating myself to items of clothing or whatever else was desired, instead of depriving myself or feeling a lack of deserving. Doing this inner work was the most difficult of all, as it literally involved a process of de-programming old beliefs that had pretty much been cemented into my psyche. That little voice from ego wouldn't accept these changes readily. "Who do you think you are? You don't deserve success. You're wrong! This will never work." And there were many more ego beliefs that surfaced during this process of mental and emotional de-programming.

At times the voice of ego, that disruptor and agitator, was loud and clear. Other times it simmered until finally it could no longer hold back. Ego certainly reminded me of all that I'd left behind; the comfortable house, two income family and secure teaching career. Luckily though, my intuition kept at me, guiding and affirming at every possible opportunity. The voices in my head never forced but encouraged my endeavours every time I sought confirmation. Needless to say, confirmation was sought continually, often on a daily basis or even countless times daily. Overcoming lack of self-worth could not, and would not, be an easy task nor would it happen overnight.

Finally the big day came. I was no longer an employee of the bureaucracy. It was with excitement, trepidation and hesitation that my healing practice commenced. There is a commonly known fact that generally it takes three years for a business to become successful or to break even financially. There is most definitely a grain of truth to that fact. Financially the first year was a disaster. Confidence wise it was a success. My belief in myself and my abilities grew exponentially through the many opportunities that occurred.

It felt as though I had found my niche in the world. Suddenly I met more like-minded individuals. Many of them were highly artistic or creative in some way. All, like me, were seeking to find deeper meaning within. The personalities were diverse and colourful. My interest in the esoteric, metaphysical and unexplainable continued to be explored and my appetite whetted. This was more meaningful than anything I'd learned during all those years spent chained to the formal education system.

The feelings of guilt, shame or always being wrong were gradually eased from my emotional being. I was with my tribe. It was not necessary to seek validation or acceptance from them. There was a generosity of spirit, a natural sharing and mutual understanding among us.

In this group I found what the Dalai Lama described in his book *Ancient Wisdom Modern World: Ethics for the New Millennium.* These people were my spiritual peers. At one stage in the book the Dalai Lama described at length the difference between being religious and being spiritual. Being spiritual is an inner experience, one that doesn't require set teachings or dogma. It can be experienced anywhere and anytime. There is no attendance required in a place of shared worship. No one dictates the credo by which you live. And so much more. Phew, finally the sense of belonging felt stronger. At the same time self-acceptance was also strengthened due to the ceaseless mantras recited and self-honouring activities. It felt good. Life was satisfying.

"If you don't like something change it; if you can't change it, change the way you think about it."

Maryu Engelbreit

CHAPTER 7

"Have you ever been sexually abused?"

"No, never".

What an unexpected question to be asked. It just happened to be asked numerous times by various practitioners. Almost every time I lay on the massage table for a Reiki or spiritual healing session that question would surface, expressed in its many different forms. To be asked such a question once wasn't cause for concern but to be asked by several people at unrelated times was unsettling.

One person persisted with the questioning. "Are you sure you haven't been molested?"

"No, am not sure. But if that's the case then I have absolutely no recollection of it happening. Why do you ask that question?" was my puzzled response.

"I'm feeling it in your body. It feels like that you were abused at some time in your life."

Memories surfaced of what Sam had shared when he was massaging my body. "Every body tells a story". What was my body emitting? If I'd been sexually abused then when had it happened? And even more frightening, who was the perpetrator? Was there only one perpetrator or had there been multiple incidents? Most importantly, why couldn't I remember? Surely something as significant and traumatic as this wouldn't be forgotten. Besides, sexual abuse was something that happened to other people. It could never happen to me.

If there's one thing I've learned it's that the more an answer to a puzzling question is sought the more elusive is the answer. This question plagued me for hours, days, weeks and months. Reflections on my life, from the earliest times I could remember were focused on and dissected. I was like a bloodhound, on the scent of something but unable to find where that scent was leading me. By this stage I'd undertaken a significant amount of inner healing of old pain to realize that I'd been subjected to both emotional and mental abuse, and that this abuse whether intentional or not had resulted in deep trauma to my psyche. Healing the trauma of abuse is a long-term process involving the release of many layers of pain memory. The possibility of sexual abuse being added to the mix was almost unbearable.

It was the middle of the night. My bladder was screaming for release. Half asleep I stumbled to the bathroom. It was only as I fumbled my way back to bed in the dark that a jolt went through my body. The dream! I had to write it down immediately as I knew that it would be forgotten in the morning otherwise. The dream was vivid and stark. It answered the unanswered question; the question that I'd been hoping had been without substance. I had been sexually violated at a very young age. There had been no penetration only inappropriate touching. The perpetrator was my father. I felt sickened beyond belief.

Once that chink in my memory opened up there were further memories. Repulsive memories of my father's erection, of his fondling and more. I remembered vivid dreams I'd had at different times, all involving my father and each time I had woken from sleep I'd dismissed those dream memories as being gross and untenable. Obviously my subconscious had been attempting to tell me something. At the age of thirteen he'd inappropriately touched my developing breasts in a very intimate manner. At that stage I'd had no hesitation in telling him to stay the hell away from me. Throughout my life he'd shared too much about his own sexual needs and frustrations and every time that happened I'd felt sick to my stomach. This wasn't normal had been my reasoning. What parent in their right mind shared this kind of intimate information with their child?

The subtle signs of sexual abuse had been there all along. Only I hadn't seen them or certainly hadn't joined the dots to see the bigger picture. To think that this devout Catholic, who preached righteous living and the dangers of sin, was most likely a frustrated paedophile didn't sit too well with me. Sickening emotions of violation roiled deep within. The urge to vomit arose. If only it were that simple to purge the mish-mash of ugly emotions that surfaced.

The worst part of all was I had no one to talk to about this revelation. Memory recall was many years after the fact. Yet my body's visceral response was strong confirmation of what had transpired. The lucid dream was no mirage or mistake. The shaking in my body continued for some days. Then rage surfaced. I spewed intense anger for weeks afterwards. Anger at the violation, at the abuse of trust, at the hypocrisy I'd heard all my life. Hatred for my father and his actions surfaced.

Confronting the reality of this abuse was probably one of the toughest challenges yet. Daily I walked long distances. Focusing on my breath I'd visualize breathing in white light and breathing out dark, yucky, crappy memories. Deep and focused breath work helped ease the pain and anger within. It also meant that innocent friends and total strangers were not subjected to outbursts of misdirected rage. My anger was volcanic at that stage, liable to erupt over the slightest misperceived comment or issue. Deep down I realized that this anger being expressed was the anger that had been stored within for nearly fifty years. It had been suppressed, packed down and ignored because I'd learned from a very early age that it was not beneficial to my wellbeing to express strong emotions.

The deep anger took months to finally ease and for acceptance to seep in. Obviously one of my life challenges was to heal the energy of abuse within, which was why I'd been on the receiving end of different kinds of abuse. There is a saying in metaphysical circles that "what we resist persists". Being highly sensitive I'd been on the receiving end of verbal, mental and emotional abuse for practically all my life. The patterning of abuse was evident in so many areas of my life as I tormented myself with endless replays, questions and reflections.

There are plenty of stories about women who are abused by their partners. It's not easy to break the cycle of abuse, which is why if a woman is able to leave an abusive relationship the only way to ensure that another abusive relationship isn't formed is to heal that abuse energy. It's a vibe that permeates every cell in the body. As Sam had said years earlier "Every body tells a story". My story was one of abuse and so during the course of my life I'd attracted abuse in its many forms, including eventually self-abuse, which manifested as lack of self love and worth as a human being. In order to clear and heal the abuse energy it's important to deal honestly with the issues, and to eventually undertake forgiveness work. It's a journey, one that is fraught with painful memories, strong emotions and requires grit and determination.

The last thing I'd been expecting when setting out on my own, seeing clients and creating a new and fulfilling life was to be confronted with sexual abuse memories. It felt as though no matter which way I turned there were further stumbling blocks to contend with. On a crisp, sunny and clear morning's walk along the beach I grumbled to my invisible, non-physical friends. As always they understood and quickly put my mind at ease. Life just felt really hard. Despite the positive things happening there always seemed to be something that arose to challenge me to the core.

"Why does it have to be so difficult? Why, for just once, can't my life be simple and easy?" I moaned.

"How can you understand if you have not experienced," were the words I heard clearly in my head.

Darnation! Here I was hoping for a break but instead immediately had a knowing that in order to be a better than average practitioner I needed to understand fully what my clients experienced. It seemed that being an observer, rather than an active participant in life, wasn't going to be an option. In order to fully relate on every level my sensitivity and empathy were going to be fully honed to the utmost degree. Ironically I also immediately intuited that no matter whatever challenges I would experience in future the emotional impact of those responses would be of my choice.

Being a victim was one possible option. Not happening. Another would be to go into denial and suppress any and all emotions. Never again. Or, the more painful but healthier option would be to have the experience and learn from it as quickly as possible. Worrying or over thinking an issue or situation would only worsen the impact. Instead, allowing it and thanking the experience as an opportunity for growth and learning would immediately lessen the pain while simultaneously supporting understanding.

All this sounds absolutely ideal in theory. Putting it into practice would be an entirely different thing. The pain of bringing the sexual abuse emotion to the surface had been excruciating. It was definitely not something I ever wished to re-experience. So possibly here was another, equally powerful though less painful way of dealing with any similar emotional issues that would surface in the future.

One issue around the sexual abuse revelations remained for many years, much to my surprise. There was deep shame and reluctance to admit to anyone that this had happened. In particular, family and close friends were not told. There were two reactions I wasn't willing to accept. The first was denial, being told that I was mistaken and that my father was not that kind of man. The second was pity. Dealing with comments along the lines of, "Oh you poor thing. What a horrible thing to have happen." Then to be questioned about what had happened or how I could trust what I'd come to know was, to my reckoning, merely dredging up what I'd already had to deal with and had no desire to continually resuscitate the story. It was easier to remain quiet and to deal with the pain and grief in my own way.

One of the things that quickly became apparent in my client work is that often quite a number of clients would come with similar issues. At this particular time it became evident that the issue of sexual violation wasn't going to fade into the background as I'd hoped. Instead, many of my clients in the coming months had experienced sexual abuse, including rape by family members. It turned out that there were far more horrific stories than mine, that sexual abuse in all its connotations was far more commonplace than I'd thought. In working with clients I found my own healing took place.

Here I could be fully honest with myself and them when I said, "I understand," because I fully understood and empathised with their experience and perceptions of that experience. In some ways I eventually realized that my own abuse experiences were a gift. In understanding others' situations I not only healed but believe I became a better practitioner. My work felt enriched by this. It also taught me the importance of detachment and compassion. I understood fully without taking on the emotions of others. In the understanding I was also able to assist others into accepting what had happened to them and to guide and support them out of victim mode and into a gradual state of self-empowerment, wherever possible.

A few years later I was summoned to my father's death bed. It was a shock to see him, a mere shadow of the tall and robust man he'd once been. His body ravaged by illness; he looked very aged and frail. The medical chart at the end of the bed said Nil by Mouth, indicating that the only sustenance he was receiving was morphine, used to deaden the pain. It would be lying to say that I felt compassion, which would have been the right thing for a spiritual person to feel. I wasn't that generous. Instead I felt nothing, absolutely nothing. The whole family was there, many family members I'd not seen for some time. My father looked up as I walked in and after several minutes his eyes found mine.

"I was a right bastard to you," he said.

"I forgive you," was my response. And I had.

Those were the only words uttered between us. The exchange wasn't noticed or understood by anyone else in the crowded hospital room. The truth of the matter was that I felt nothing; it was as though all the pain of the abuse and the years of living in the family home with his anger, strictures and rantings no longer had any hold over me. I truly had forgiven, but that didn't mean I'd ever forget.

Not that long after his death I came across some information shared by medical intuitive Carolyn Myss. One story or explanation she offered strongly resonated and helped me finally put the energy of abuse behind me in ways I'd not done previously. Earlier I'd read that on a soul level we all plan our life prior to incarnating into a human body. My reaction when first encountering this particular information was, "What the hell was I thinking?" I just couldn't believe my stupidity!

Carolyn Myss explained it simply in story book form, or that is how I came to view and understand what was an otherwise complex concept. The basis of this explanation was that prior to incarnating the soul (Soul X) met up with soul family members. Soul X might indicate that this next lifetime would be about learning forgiveness, or to experience addiction, abuse, to learn some positive or negative experiences around finances, or something else of importance to Soul X. At this meeting of soul family members different souls would become involved in the process, with one soul indicating that they would incarnate as a parent, another as a relationship partner, another as a friend, and so on. Each of these souls would then have the specific purpose of assisting Soul X achieve its purpose, and that this whole process is undertaken with unconditional love. The eventual purpose of this process ultimately being the growth and learning of Soul X. This is the process by which the soul can evolve into higher levels of consciousness. Possibly this is a simplistic explanation of a highly complex process or situation, but nevertheless it need not be discounted.

To the average mind this explanation may defy logic and even seem absurd. However, it's obvious that within society there are individuals who are referred to as 'old souls', and others who are obviously 'young souls'. If there's one thing I've learned it's that as implausible as some things may sound initially all too often there's a kernel of truth in many explanations. The Carolyn Myss explanation, while simplistic, in a nutshell provided peace of mind and understanding that otherwise would be impossible to find. With the understanding came acceptance. Rather than feeling life was painfully tough, that abuse and I were too closely intertwined it was time to move on from that energy. I understood its purpose, and that purpose was to guide me to a space of true self love and acceptance.

"A mind that is stretched by a new experience can never go back to its old dimensions."

Oliver Wendell Holmes

CHAPTER 8

A weekend class on colours, their meaning and impact looked interesting and different to anything previously experienced. My intention was to learn what felt appropriate and to also enjoy time with a group of strangers; maybe even explore the possibility of a small thread of creativity lurking deep within. It was a small gathering, which was perfectly suitable. My training had not been in the creative arts and while I realistically didn't expect to discover any hidden talent nevertheless I was open to all opportunities.

Carol, the facilitator, was warm hearted and enthusiastic about colours, their meaning and significance in our lives. Various activities, lots of discussion and sharing were the theme of the two day workshop. Our own personalities were also analysed, based on sketches and colour preferences. This analysis occurred on the second day and was given in a one on one situation. To this day only two points made by Carol remain etched in my memory. They remain because I did not want to hear or acknowledge them, and everything else she said over the course of the weekend was immediately forgotten.

"You are a channel and you are also an alien," came the bald statement.

I was stunned and disbelieving. My reaction was to pull away and say nothing. Denial is a funny thing. It can arise as an immediate reaction or may take time to filter through to the conscious. My non-verbal response was instantaneous and I went into vehement mental denial.

"As much as you may wish to deny this it's not possible. The sooner you accept this the easier it will be," she continued. Obviously she had picked up on my intense and even hostile reaction to her statement.

So much for knowing that I'd come from a far off constellation or that I'd always known home wasn't here. That awareness was something to hold onto from a distance. It was a personal knowing. Being told outright by someone who didn't know me was extremely unsettling. There was only one way to respond and that was to forget the conversation had ever occurred. A part of me still hadn't fully accepted my differences and I had no intention of broadening my skills to include channelling or considering myself as being an alien. On a deeper level I was still coming to terms with the fact that I didn't fit into the mainstream beliefs about what was deemed normal. That didn't mean I was ready to be viewed as an oddball or eccentric. On some subtle or sub-conscious level appearances were still important. But I should have known better than to think I could hide my oddities behind a demeanour of normality or that other people would be unable to see those differences.

Once I'd left the employee workforce opportunities abounded with rapid frequency and in many directions. Suddenly it felt as though I'd taken on a juggling act. New interests, new people and new learning all occurred with a rapidity that was totally unexpected.

Meditation became a big part of my daily routine, often meditating up to an hour both morning and night. During meditation I consistently felt a twirling sensation arise out of my crown (head) chakra and before I knew it felt myself travelling to distant constellations where learning, exploration and adventures occurred. These meditation experiences were reminiscent of those adventures experienced as a very young girl. I was re-connecting with my spirit family once I went into alpha state and from there into the deeper theta meditative state. Other times I felt spirit energies alongside my body and mental dialogue would occur. These visitations provided ample opportunity for my non-stop questioning about the meaning of reality, about creation and all that existed beyond the three dimensional reality on this planet.

When discussing meditation practice with friends and colleagues it seemed that my meditations were vastly different from the norm. Guided meditations, where a facilitator would take students into a beautiful garden or forest didn't work. Every time I attempted to follow someone else's guided directions the same thing would happen. I'd swirl out of my body, via the crown chakra and find myself out in the inky darkness where lights would be twinkling in the distance, and from there further adventures would await me. Despite the different meditation techniques attempted and the determination to experience what others experienced it just didn't happen. It had become apparent that even my meditation technique and experiences were somewhat out of the normal range as described by other people I knew who engaged successfully in regular practice.

Luckily Transcendental Meditation looked like it might offer a way of meditating successfully and in a more normally acceptable manner. With this in mind I attended an information meeting on Transcendental Meditation that was held locally. During the meeting we were told about the importance of meditating the Transcendental Meditation way. Any other way was dangerous, though no real explanation as to why it was dangerous was given. In addition, we would be given our special meditation sound symbol. It all sounded interesting and well thought out. The audience certainly seemed interested.

It looked as though there would have been a number of people signing up for the expensive course until I began asking questions. The clincher question was lengthy and convoluted.

"In Transcendental Meditation you acknowledge that we all live many lifetimes?"

"Yes."

"If that's the case then surely every person brings a vast sub-conscious memory of other life experiences into this one?"

The response was then a slight nod.

"If that's the case then surely it's likely that many individuals would have experience with meditation, serious religious or esoteric experiences and more from other lifetimes?"

This time the slight nod was even slighter.

"Then how come in Transcendental Meditation there's only one way to meditate, that other ways are considered to be unsafe, possibly dangerous or irrelevant? The point I'm making is that surely memories of these practices from other lifetimes can be carried through to this lifetime and could be as relevant," came the final part to my question that wasn't really a question.

As we walked out of the venue it looked like there would be no sign ups for the Transcendental Meditation training program that evening. It wasn't my intention to create disruption or uncertainty to the session. All I sought was clarification around the validity of my own meditation experiences. After that information session I accepted that my meditations were uniquely mine, worked perfectly and need not be adapted to any other model.

During this time I continued working with clients, meditating and listening to the wisdom and guidance of my spirit guides. These guides were the invisible, non-physical beings that were with me twenty-four seven. Often I saw them clairvoyantly though most times I felt their presence strongly. I asked questions, they replied. Often responses were not as I'd prefer or even anticipated. Nevertheless the amount of learning from these encounters was astronomical. I learned more from the dialogues than could ever have been gleaned from reading the countless books I'd been devouring voraciously. My attitude began to shift. Reading books involved reading about someone else's experiences and understanding of those experiences. Getting it directly from the horse's mouth, so to speak, was a privilege.

A significant part of learning involved becoming discerning in the interactions with spirit guides, or non-physical beings. How could I be assured that these entities were there for my highest good? Was it possible to be taken over by entities that were malevolent? How could that be prevented? Most of the books I'd read seemed to focus only on the good guys, the archangels and more. My questioning centred on the purpose of duality due to the fact that we live in a world where there is both evil and good, and where aspects of duality are evident in everyday existence.

One of my psychic abilities, intuition to the nth degree, was to know. Learning to trust that knowing fully wasn't difficult as I'd known stuff ever since I was young. It was when I ignored the knowing that things went pear shaped. Another psychic ability was that of being clairsentient. This involved feeling things intuitively, and which also meant being highly empathic. It was this clairsentience that stood me in good stead during this intense training period. Each spirit guide that came into my life during this period had an energy signature. This meant that its vibration felt a certain way, and was easy for me to discern it readily as it neared my body. Each different vibration eventually became easy to differentiate, and I soon realized that each spirit guide had a specific purpose and information to share.

The emotional pain in my body had reduced somewhat by then. However, intuitively I knew that there were still many layers needing to be healed and released. These layers came from many lifetimes and from transgenerational patterning. My reasoning and understanding at this particular time was still very much in its infancy, still in the process of evolving. Nevertheless in my communication with spirit guides I strongly expressed the need to cleanse myself of the heavier emotional energies I sensed still sat deeply embedded within. During meditation I asked and commanded that this be released. For some unknown reason I needed to feel clean and clear of emotional, mental, physical and spiritual debris that was preventing me from being the real me. As crazy as this may sound it was very real on a deeper, unexplainable level.

From time to time I would be guided to sit perfectly still in a chair. Posture was important. Sitting erect and upright I felt what seemed to be a strong electrical current coursing through my head and all the way down through my body. This flow of energy would continue for anywhere from thirty to sixty minutes on average. Instinctively I knew this was powerful cosmic healing energy that would support my request to clear all the debris that was sitting within my being. The sensations were fantastic, better than any drug induced high. Ironically I'd never done drugs, wasn't interested in them as I was a firm believer that meditation was the way to inner peace and harmony.

For several days after such a session energy levels would be high and mental clarity amazing. I felt fantastic on every level, almost as though I'd been super-charged. Then suddenly, after about a week, I'd feel as though I'd been run over by a Mack truck. Every muscle and joint in my body ached horrifically. Exhaustion and non-functioning pervaded every cell. Extreme tiredness, mental fog combined with emotional reactivity also reigned supreme for several days. Then suddenly those horrible, even debilitating, symptoms would disappear and I'd definitely feel lighter, calmer and clearer within.

After the first reaction to the energy clearing flow I mentally asked, "What happened? Why do I feel so sick and exhausted?"

"You asked for it," I heard in my head. And I had, asked for it that is. In a meditation I had commanded that all the deep seated "crap" be removed, cleared and released. That simple request had produced an outcome that I'd not anticipated. Surprisingly it never occurred that asking for the release to be gentle might be an easier option. As time went on and more of the energy clearing flows occurred my body's response became less intense, though there was always some form of residual discomfort and tiredness experienced.

Loose knit friendship groups were formed during this time. One such group met regularly to undertake Reiki and spiritual healing on one another. During these sessions I found it interesting to hear channelled messages delivered by other group members. The messages were interesting and certainly seemed relevant to whatever was happening at any particular time. Was I sceptical? Was it really possible to bring in an entity energy and have it speak through one's vocal cords? By this stage I'd read most of Jane Roberts books, where she'd channelled fascinating scientific information from an entity she referred to as Seth. I'd also read a book about the life of Edgar Cayce and his experiences as a trance channel.

While I was comfortable with and enjoyed the mental dialogue with non-physical friends that didn't necessarily mean I was prepared to actually allow my body to be taken over by an entity for channelling purposes. It may have been possible that all those earlier dire warnings from Christian friends about such dangers had seeped into my sub-conscious. Having an energy take over my being could mean possession, something I definitely wasn't willing to allow. Alas, conscious intention and what is meant to be often collide. Some things that are meant to be will happen irrespective of conscious will or decisiveness. In other words, resistance was futile.

It happened one evening as this particular small group was gathered for another session of healing and sharing. One participant had channelled a short piece. As she was doing this I felt a distinct energy presence to one side of my body. This invisible presence was strong and very warm and it was pushing into my body. Possibly every fear I still possessed surfaced instinctively. Others in the group saw what was happening and were extremely encouraging. On some level I knew that it was going to happen despite any ego resistance on my part. Gently the group guided me through the process, sharing that the entity was of the Light, that it was time for me to begin doing what I was meant to be doing, which was to be a channel for spiritual information.

The sensations were unfamiliar and overwhelming. The pressure intensified. My body temperature felt like it was increasing rapidly. It literally felt like another being was taking full possession of my body, slowly and steadily. I was guided to let the conscious aspect of myself step outside my body as this would make the process easier. Each step of the way was painstaking and frightening. It had become commonplace to spiral out of my body during meditation and also to consciously astral travel to places, as I'd done when much younger. This, however, was a totally different sensation, and it wasn't comfortable. By the time this particular entity had settled within my body, the conscious energy aspect of myself was outside at what felt like an acute angle to my body. It felt as though my human body was about to topple over despite the fact that the physical aspect of myself was standing erect at right angles to the floor.

Before I could think or say anything there was a strong tingling, and even burning sensation in my throat. The desire to cough was strong. My mouth began moving with that gaping movement common to fish once they're out of water. Involuntary speech, in a voice totally unfamiliar and unrecognizable was the next surprise. Haltingly word after word erupted strongly and clearly. This was not a voice I knew. It wasn't my voice, or the words of my conscious expression. It was only a brief channelling and then gently the entity slid out of my body, leaving me feeling exhausted and crumbling in a heap. The support from the group was incredible. There were plenty of reassurances. The channelled message made sense. I had absolutely no idea what had been said nor was there any recall later on either. Apparently there was some truth to Carol's words. Despite my denial and resistance channelling was going to be part of my spiritual journey. It was an inescapable fact.

Another understanding also surfaced. Those amazing cosmic energy downloads were essential to the channelling process. Spirit beings of high vibration cannot, and will not, enter the human body that holds low vibration. The mental, emotional and spiritual pain held within the human energy field interferes with the connection and prevents the purity of higher frequency messages. In order to become a clear channel my body needed to be clear of debris that impeded the transmission. Ego definitely needed to be minimized and relegated to the background.

"*The mind can accept any boundary anywhere. But the reality is that, by its very nature, existence cannot have any boundary because what will be beyond the boundary – again another sky. Skies upon skies are available for your flight. Don't be content easily…*"

Osho

CHAPTER 9

From an early age schooling had been easy. Lessons, often boring and seemingly irrelevant, were usually straightforward. Homework was something to be endured. Education in everyday life entailed book learning and regurgitation. Tests and essays were marked right or wrong depending on which prescribed books had been read and digested. Simply understanding exactly what was required meant getting decent assignment results. I'd learned that it was basically a matter of playing the game in order to succeed. Though, of course, I often wondered what the hell was meant by the words 'succeed' and 'successful'. Who or what were the arbiters of deciding this? What were the parameters defining that a person succeeded or was successful? Eventually, rather than analysing and feeling a great deal of frustration at what I perceived to be a draconian education system I chose to opt out, no longer believing in all that I'd been taught. In the process it was more comfortable and reliable to trust intuition and to relegate logic and reasoning to three dimensional reality.

The non-physical spirit guides didn't teach me. They enabled my learning, they facilitated exploration and understanding. There was never a right or wrong answer, there were choices or options. I learned that all actions or non-actions produce outcomes; I learned that thoughts, emotions and intentions are as powerful as action or non-action. Those early years of working intensely and closely with spirit guides were my formative years, which provided a wealth of experience and knowledge. The breadth of this far exceeded any tertiary studies I'd previously undertaken. The meaningfulness of these formative years remains etched within and formed the basis or foundation of who I was still to become. Along the way, however, there were plenty of concepts to explore and learn, numerous choices to be corrected, and countless changes in direction. If the first half of my life had been relatively predictable and monotonous then the second half was anything but. It was the exact opposite.

From the very beginning of real spiritual awakening I'd been aware of the difference between light and dark spirit energies. Instinctively I felt it was important to only work with Light beings, those whose energy frequency was one of service and enlightenment. I wasn't interested in black magic, curses, spells, Ouija boards or anything along those lines. Still, I was aware that there's a fine line dividing the two. Over emphasis on ego drive and personal satisfaction has the potential to shift energy from light to dark very easily. The memory of the deep black entities that had attempted possession a couple of years earlier in numerous hotel rooms remained firmly etched in mind. That memory entailed violation, control and ultimately lack of self-empowerment.

Thus, the choice was easy. While my intuitive discernment felt healthy there was still quite a lengthy process of learning to be undergone. Accessing written information about such things wasn't fruitful. The literature on exorcism and the black arts was more readily available, but not relevant to my needs. Instead I relied on intuition or inner knowing. This involved communicating with the spirit beings that came into contact, checking that they came with light and that they held light. If there was one thing I quickly learned it's that there are mischievous spirits out there who happily will lie about themselves in order to fool unsuspecting individuals. The truth, though, is that they are unable to maintain that façade; their lies quickly become apparent and it's simply a matter of ordering them to leave.

I'd also gotten into the habit of putting in place a protective shield around my aura or energy field. Nowadays scientists confirm that energy from one person interacts with that of others, in much the same way as happens with plants and animals. Back then this was a commonly known fact among the metaphysical and spiritual community. There was often discussion, even debate as to whether or not it was necessary to place a protective shield around one's energy field. Some individuals insisted that when you come from a position of love then no protection at all is needed. At that stage this claim made sense though I still wasn't fully convinced. On another morning walk along the beach I questioned my spirit guides about the need, or otherwise, of putting in energetic protective shields.

since I'd cried. It took time for the ability to cry to re-emerge. The first time it happened I was shocked, and then relieved to know that it was possible. In the first year or so after leaving the marriage it wasn't easy to cry and whenever it happened it was accompanied by pain so deep that I felt its release from deep within my abdomen. Now, about eight years later crying came more easily. Being demonstrative and affectionate or sharing my deepest feelings was still somewhat of a challenge. There was still too much emotion being stuffed down, though not from lack of conscious intention and effort to be more spontaneous and open.

The real change occurred after the meditation where brain integration and mind expansion had taken place. Slowly and steadily the changes became evident. Instead of zipping the lips words would pop out of my mouth, expressing some feeling or emotion that once would have been left unuttered. I became a hugger. Clients and friends were on the receiving end of this newfound expression of affection. When recounting stories or experiences it was no longer difficult to explain emotions. I became comfortable with owning my emotions and allowing them to be evident to others. It was a massive liberation.

"The one who follows the crowd will usually go no further than the crowd. Those who walk alone are likely to find themselves in places no one has ever been before."

Albert Einstein

CHAPTER 10

It was a relief to feel more comfortable around people. Maybe this was due to the fact that the stream of new acquaintances was of a similar ilk. Friendships forged felt deeper and more meaningful. The ease of conversation was a noticeable improvement; it was definitely a work in progress. I was no longer being chided or reminded of the dangers inherent in my new field of interest. Clients frequently confided their weird experiences with paranormal phenomena. It was surprising just how many so-called ordinary people had had unusual, frightening or paranormal encounters. These were far more commonplace than I'd ever thought possible. What became apparent is that it's normal to have such experiences, and that the most usual reaction is to keep them secret for fear of derision and scorn.

This opening up and feeling more comfortable in conversation didn't mean I shared all my unusual or paranormal incidents. When shared with close friends often only an abbreviated or simplified version was related. This was due to the fact that my experiences and interactions were intensely personal and it had become apparent that some of them were well outside the realm of ordinariness, even in the metaphysical world where often anything goes. Around this time I began channelling to clients during sessions. Information channelled generally related to their life purpose and explored the nature of issues encountered in this particular lifetime.

Many psychic mediums are gifted at bringing information from loved ones on the other side. Often a loved parent, grandparent, friend, sibling or others who have crossed bring insight and share wisdom. That wasn't my kind of channelling. It's never been that way. The beings I channel are spirit guides and aliens. This doesn't mean that aliens aren't spirit guides, they often are. To this day I still am leery of the word 'alien' when describing non-physical beings from elsewhere. From day one they've been my space brothers and sisters and continue to remain as such.

In the middle of a massage, Reiki or spiritual healing session I'd feel a warm buzzing around my body. I would remain completely still, going into a relaxed state or zone and then words would tumble out. Initially it was simple messages, often providing clarification or confirmation for client needs. From there the channelling expanded to include friendship gatherings, where I would effortlessly slip from having ordinary conversation into the light trance mode necessary for channelling. Generally I did not remember what had been shared, or when I did it was only small snippets that remained in my consciousness. This was a comfortable existence, a lifestyle that was diverse, interesting and where ongoing learning was the norm. It was the ideal niche to remain comfortable in because for the first time in my life I felt at home with myself, with friends and with my newfound career. That feeling of ease didn't last too long unfortunately.

Despite some of the confrontational challenges with the dark forces my personal and social life continued expanding with ample opportunities for meeting and sharing with other like-minded individuals. At one such instance the dinner party was well in progress. It was held at a friend's place. I knew some of the guests, many of whom were on a similar wavelength in terms of interests and understanding. Sitting there, enjoying the company and the delicious meal I suddenly felt that all too familiar warmth to one side of my body.

"Not now!" I mentally hissed.

The nudging continued, getting stronger and stronger.

"I'm not channelling. It's not appropriate," was my strong protest. This nudging and resistance continued back and forth for quite a while. As always, resistance was futile though normally there was mutual agreement regarding my availability and the appropriateness of channelling.

Before I could control my mouth a strong masculine sounding voice boomed out, immediately attracting everyone's attention. It was definitely not an energy that I'd channelled previously. It spoke for some time about the coming times, about the disasters and potential destruction of the planet. It wasn't a lengthy channelling, but certainly long enough for my public image as being somewhat 'eccentrically normal' to be totally shattered and in ruins. The reaction among the guests was one of either fright or shock. I was mortified, apologized profusely and needless to say was among the first guests to leave.

Apparently, despite all the inner work undertaken on self-acceptance, there was still more to do. A part of me still craved to be seen as 'normal', maybe not exactly the same normal as everyone else but still somewhere within the wider range of what is perceived to be acceptable. Judging by the responses of some of the guests at the dinner party my behaviour was totally out of the normal range. Some damage control was needed. Over the next few days there was considerable mental dialogue with spirit guides.

Apparently it was time to fully accept the role of being a channel, and for that role to extend beyond the previously safe or limited domain. There was still a lot of work ahead, with channelling being a significant part of my future role, so I was told. The beings who had been channelled indicated they were unprepared for the level of fear that surfaced from within the guests at the dinner party. At that time they had felt massive waves of fear surfacing from the guests, which was surprising given that in general the level of understanding and awareness of the group was higher than is often the case within most social groups.

Overall the damage to my reputation was nil, or minimal at most. There was questioning and curiosity about what had happened, how I'd come to be a channel, what it involved and so on. All this came about later once the shock of the incident had abated. Ultimately the incident served me well, propelling me further forward in my search for understanding. It was time to accept the fact that my origins are alien in nature. That being the case it was then essential to learn more about space brothers and sisters from other constellations, and to begin identifying exactly the nature of my origins. So began a lengthy search, one where there were many false flags and misdirection taken.

∞∞∞∞

It was a casual conversation with someone I'd only just met at another social event. This person mentioned several names and upon hearing one particular lady's name I knew I had to meet her. Phone call and arrangements to meet were made effortlessly. Upon turning up at her door I saw this petite, very slender lady with a mop of white curls and the most brilliant smile.

Once inside she said, "Are you wanting a reading or a healing?"

"Neither, I just knew we needed to meet."

"Oh, you're right. We do."

That was the beginning of a deep friendship lasting more than ten years, and extending beyond this lifetime once she transitioned to the other side. Daisy was one in a million. She embraced her uniqueness and eccentricities as though they were perfectly normal. When looking at her all I saw was light, she radiated it in spades. Her wisdom was beyond description. Understanding and acceptance were her *modus operandi*. Her psychic abilities were the sharpest and strongest I'd ever encountered. Yet despite this she lived simply, small things amused and entertained her. She did not take herself or life seriously. In time she came to remind me of the monks I'd meet in Nepal and India. She had that beautiful child-like enjoyment of life. Laughter was her best friend.

Our friendship forged strongly. Daisy became my second mother, the mother I'd never had. She knew by the tone of my voice when something was out of kilter; she read me like a book and dispensed her inimitable kindness and wisdom in ways that my soul craved. Daisy was my mentor and teacher also. Her teaching was based on story-telling and sharing, and was always accompanied by plenty of laughter. It was thanks to her guidance and understanding that my journey wasn't as complicated, painful or terrifying as it would otherwise have been. Here was a like-minded soul, one who had learned from her spirit guides and who had learned to trust that particular brand of tuition rather than relying on book learning.

Daisy astral travelled through the universe and saw vistas so great that most psychics would never hope to see in their lifetime. She also saw aliens, communicated with them and felt extremely comfortable being around these non-physical beings.

Daisy also happened to be a people magnet. She attracted people and animals constantly. Stray animals always found a haven in her home and garden. Wild birds flocked to her. And she was able to communicate with all creatures, long before it became publicly acknowledged that animal communicators actually can do what they claim.

At one social gathering where Daisy was sharing more of her fascinating stories she suddenly turned and looked at me. "You are so ugly. If you could see the real you then you'd know what I'm talking about," and then she cackled her wicked laugh. I immediately knew she was referring to my alien form, the one that was hidden beneath my physical body. We all laughed because with Daisy there was no malice, only honesty. If ever I'd needed confirmation of my alien roots that was it. Daisy never lied, she didn't make up stories. Truth, often when bluntly spoken has a strong tone, one which cannot be ignored.

Many years later when living overseas I awoke early one morning and saw her spirit standing beside my bed. "Daisy, what are you doing here?" As the question was asked I knew she had transitioned and she'd come to say goodbye.

"It's so beautiful here," she said excitedly. "If you could only see what I see. It's so much better seeing it from this side than from your side," were her final words. Daisy was like a child at a birthday party. I saw and felt her eagerness. That communication was cut short by the phone ringing. A friend back in Australia said, "I have something to tell you."

"I know. Daisy is here, she's been telling me about her new adventure."

Daisy's gift was invaluable. Thanks to her acceptance, teaching and understanding I came to recognize and accept my own uniqueness. All those idiosyncrasies and differences had become internalized and normalized in the years I had the privilege of knowing Daisy.

∞∞∞∞∞

Once the gates to intuition and psychic abilities opened up there was no stopping the flood. Despite maintaining that clairvoyance wasn't a strong ability there were phases when all I saw were future potentials for the planet. Visions would come rapidly, with one slide after another appearing in front of my eyes. None of them were particularly inspiring as they generally indicated natural disasters and destruction. To this day I'm convinced that one of the many scenes clairvoyantly seen must have been 9/11. At the time, however, it was impossible to put a time or place on any of the potential events seen.

There are times, however, when watching the news and I see the bombing destruction carried out in other lands that the scenes look remarkably familiar. Sometimes the psychic scenes would flash by rapidly and it would be impossible to have any recall or to even write down what had been clairvoyantly seen, though later of course I would speculate on whether or not having a written record would have been worthwhile.

Two days before 9/11 I became extremely ill and agitated. This was not a physical illness, rather I found myself falling into the deepest, darkest, blackest hole. The emotional pain was intense. I felt extreme anguish and was unable to do anything other than take a shower in the middle of the day and rest. Whatever I was feeling was debilitating. Two days later recognition registered. The so-called illness was merely due to being massively swamped with the pain of the event. Once the cause registered within my consciousness I became intensely angry and railed at my spirit guides. They had told me many times that there was a lot for me to complete in this lifetime so my frustration at becoming immobilized was fierce. That it had happened was totally unacceptable, to my way of thinking anyhow.

I ranted, "How am I supposed to carry out my life purpose if I become overcome by the emotional pain of humanity whenever a disaster of massive proportion strikes? This is completely unacceptable. You tell me one thing and yet expect my human body to function irrespective of how badly it's impacted!" Undoubtedly I said a lot more, most of it unprintable. By this stage the relationship had become well established and I was quite comfortable about letting it be known when I was dissatisfied with something. I was certainly not averse to using strong language if the need arose. During the course of the many mental dialogues I'd been told that we had a partnership, one where I was equally powerful. Well, most times I was aware that wasn't really the case but nevertheless recognized that like a young child learning to walk I also needed to exert my spiritual muscle from time to time.

During meditation a couple of days later I clairvoyantly saw a large cylinder being placed around my aura or energy field. Its colour was a blueish grey and it looked like it had Swiss cheese patterning. This made absolutely no sense and despite my questioning no answer was forthcoming as to its function or purpose. About a week later I caught up with a colleague and during our conversation mentioned what had happened.

"Ah, that's a Faraday Cage," he said.

"A what?"

"It's what's used in recording studios, where musicians inside the studio are unable to hear what's going on outside, but those on the outside can hear whatever is going on inside. It would appear that you've been given a strong protective shield, which should ensure that you no longer feel things so intensely."

He was correct. Since that time there have been countless disasters, natural or manmade that would elicit deep compassion within, yet not once has there been a repeat of that intense weakening and emotional pain within.

"The cave you fear to enter holds the treasure you seek."

Joseph Campbell

CHAPTER 11

Training to be a clear channel continued regardless of whatever else happened in my life. The long intense downloads of energy that went coursing from the top of my head all the way through my body took place regularly. The high that followed never failed to stimulate my interest or generate further physical wellbeing. Earlier reactions of feeling as though I'd been hit by a Mack truck eased considerably. It got to the point where I simply felt energized immediately afterwards for a day or so and then more tired than usual for a few days after that. The tiredness was due to stress or cellular memory releasing, and I eventually realized that sometimes the body needs to rest and that during the resting phase there's often healing and integration occurring on a deeper level.

The purpose of the energy downloads continued to be for clearing out the negative energies, heavy memories and more from all lifetimes. The desire to be clear and clean within remained strong. Intuitively I knew that when the time was right I'd be a clearer channel for higher beings. Some channels work solely with one particular entity, such as Jane Roberts with Seth, Lee Carrol with Kryon or Esther Hicks with Abraham. That was not how it was meant to be in my case.

During this time I was fortunate to have some interesting and varied spirit guides; most provided guidance in my healing room while others offered assistance on a personal or spiritual level. When working with clients in my workspace it became commonplace to channel their particular guides. This basically meant that the message delivery was brief and concise. Other times those with me in spirit came through. What convinced me of the accuracy of the messages was the constant feedback provided by clients.

Ultimately I came to view spirit guides as energy holding intelligent consciousness. However in the early days it felt appropriate that each guide have a name or identity I could relate to. This was more for my own surety and conviction than anything else. For quite a long time there were numerous spirit guides from what I referred to as the Angelic Realm. As a young child I'd had an overwhelming fascination with angels, reading stories about them, drawing them and collecting angel stickers. The various and distinct energy signatures I felt from them were familiar, and felt very much like family. Different members from this collective served a different purpose in my life and in addition to recognizing their particular vibration I also knew them by their individual name.

It was during this time, meditating extensively and gaining in spiritual wisdom and understanding that the beings from the Angelic Realm played a significant role. Any channelling undertaken involving them was done in the privacy of my practice. Nowadays I'd hazard a guess that this was a period of intense training, preparing me for the more serious channelling that would follow in the coming years. Nevertheless due to the fact that I'd become extremely comfortable with their energies, I knew I could call upon them for assistance and guidance as needed. I even managed to convince myself that this was where my alien self originated from, for a while anyway.

There are times in life when upon meeting certain people there's a strong and instantaneous connection, a feeling of deep knowing and understanding them that arises. That's how it was with the spirit guides from the Angelic Realm. The feeling of comfort and ease was incredibly deep and resonated strongly. Aspects of my being astral travelled regularly to their location. I was involved in decision making and discussions relating to the whole Angelic Realm. Like my beautiful friend and mentor, Daisy, I too had learned to see out into the universe, to travel to far flung corners via astral travel and to engage where appropriate. Needless to say there were countless times when I really wasn't in my physical body, which certainly had an impact on everyday functioning. Living in two worlds or realities can be, and is, challenging and certainly interesting!

My time with the beings from the Angelic Realm eventually came to an end, as had happened with other spirit guides previously. In many ways it's simply like changing dance partners. I'd learned that different guides come in when it's time for this to happen. Obviously my time with the loving beings from the Angelic Realm needed to end and further learning and guidance was to be the responsibility of new dance partners. This time it was a collective of beings from the Arcturus constellation. Their energy felt stronger, possibly more strident, though never abrasive. The energy of the beings from the Angelic Realm had felt soft and nurturing, focussing mainly on my personal and spiritual growth. The Arcturus energy came in to provide information about the bigger picture. Their delivery was almost professional in some ways. Obviously it was time to get down to some serious business, or to ratchet up a notch with the channelling.

What I'd learned about channelling consisted of numerous Do's and Don'ts. Time had been well spent reading about it, as obviously it was happening regardless of my personal wishes. Learning about good guides and the not so good guides was part of that discernment learning process. One of the definite no-nos of channelling was that one should never channel when alone. Everything I'd read stressed the importance of always having another person present during a channelling session. Unfortunately the Arcturus Community, as I came to call them, hadn't read the How To Channel manuals.

Clear instructions were given that I needed to purchase a recording device as that would be an essential tool for the process we were about to undertake jointly. My immediate understanding was that possibly I would be channelling to one or more people and that the recording would then be transcribed. That certainly didn't happen. Instead, almost daily I was guided to meditate briefly. Then sitting in a relaxed position I switched on the old fashioned tape recording device and immediately went into a semi-trance state, channelling for thirty or more minutes at a time.

This went on day after day, first thing every morning, and certainly placed additional strain on my physical body. It wasn't long before I realized that this was why my body had been subjected to the intense energy downloads. Those electric like currents pouring through my body had been preparation for holding the higher frequency energy beings that I was now channelling on a daily basis. At the end of the day's work seeing clients I would then transcribe the channelled piece. It never ceased to amaze me. The wisdom contained within the channelling was mind blowing at times.

It became tiring work and was all consuming. There was no personal time for anything else. The channelling took priority. The days passed by in a whirl. No longer was I privy to personal information, guidance or support as had been provided by spirit guides from the Angelic Realm. This new adventure was definitely more business-like. It was demanding and non-stop.

Eventually, exhausted and overwhelmed, I held a manuscript in my hands. The Arcturus Community had requested that little or no editing be undertaken of the channelling. This posed a dilemma because the channelling was more conversational in nature and did not follow the normal structure or format of written material. In order to honour the integrity of the channelling very little editing eventually took place. My training in English and love of the written word itched to re-phrase and restructure the content, again and again. To this day I am still surprised by the amount of self-restraint exhibited. I had to remind myself that this was not my writing, these were not my words and therefore any interference by me would ruin the energy of the information provided.

The community of beings from the Arcturus constellation had initially introduced themselves one day in my workspace as I was preparing for the arrival of my first client. Clairvoyantly I saw them as extremely tall beings, very thin, pale with indistinguishable features and wearing maroon coloured cloaks. I was a bit surprised because prior to this I'd had a Chinese doctor working with me. The Chinese doctor had used phrases such as "too much yang", "too damp", or some other extremely convoluted explanation for a client's malaise or condition. While it was certainly a novelty having this Chinese spirit work with me, to this day I'll concede that my learning from his tutelage was exceedingly slim.

The Arcturians however were exceptionally different. Deferentially they introduced themselves as my new teachers. It was implicit that my agreement with this arrangement was a definite yes. By this stage I'd become very aware of my ability or prerogative to say no when something didn't feel instinctively right. It wasn't very often I exercised that option. Whenever new guidance from the non-physical realms was about to commence there were the preliminary greetings and politeness exhibited. Introductions pretty much paralleled those that take place every day in three dimension reality. This time, however, the Arcturians and I knew that those formalities were unnecessary. I was ready to progress onto the next phase of learning. Little did I realize then just how much learning would ultimately take place under their expert guidance.

As part of their brief introduction, however, they communicated that there were two conditions to the arrangement. Nowadays I really think they could just as easily have been lawyers outlining contractual terms and conditions prior to commencing work. The first condition was that I cease reading all books relating to metaphysical, spiritual or esoteric subjects. My warped sense of humour quickly saw the benefit of this being that a significant dollar fortune would be saved as a result. The second condition was that I no longer attend workshops or classes to further my education or knowledge. That condition seemed a bit far-fetched but regardless my curiosity got the better of me so I agreed wholeheartedly. These were definitely two simple conditions, which surely would be easy to comply with. There was only one glitch with this whole legally binding 'gentlemen's agreement' and that was there was no clause in the non-verbal telepathic contract as to an end date.

Thus commenced my real learning about the energetics of the human body and its healing capabilities. The fact that I'd already studied quite a bit of physiology and anatomy proved to be useful, making my understanding of their teachings easier to digest. The basis of their teaching went along these lines. Quite a number of clients would seek attention or assistance for a particular issue or condition. All I had to do was allow myself to be guided by the directions I heard in my head given at the time. At this stage I was able to see inside the human body, to see where there were energy blockages and to intuitively determine or clairvoyantly see what needed to be done to correct any particular energy blockages or impediments. In correcting these healing could then begin to occur within the client's body.

In order for learning to continue and accelerate another slew of clients would then arrive, this time with another similar issue but one of more complexity. This went on, month after month, until such time the complexity of symptoms was excessive and definitely very challenging. Interestingly, in time I came to see and understand that ultimately in practically every situation there was usually only one core issue that was the cause of all the health challenges any individual faced. In many instances clients came as a last resort due to the fact that conventional western medicine had failed. Unfortunately all too often I heard about the failures of western medicine along with the stress and cost that patients had suffered.

Many clients experienced inexplicable pains or ongoing discomfort that western medicine could find no explanation for, often despite exhaustive testing or scanning. Eventually they would be told something along the lines of, "We're not sure exactly what is going on. It might be this or that. However, just to be sure we recommend that you take this or that medication…" This was the story I heard over and over again. In many, or often most situations the so-called problem was related to the energy body, to emotional trauma such as deep fear or to a core issue that had been passed down through the family generations. The reason for the pain or on-going discomfort was energetic in nature and not physical.

One of the real challenges during this learning process was that teaching by the Arcturians was undertaken in a silent and consistent manner. My mind buzzed with questions, most of which I blurted out with monotonous frequency. Answers given ranged from, "Trust," to "You will see," and "All is well". As frustrating as this was I eventually learned that understanding would arrive in my tiny and slow human mind, in its own way and own time. The Arcturians did not provide answers. They did not teach in a manner that is familiar to our education system. Instead, the process was fully experiential. I learned through mental processing and deduction as time went on. Through such extensive training I was able to pick up and understand concepts that previously would have been difficult to absorb and digest if the learning had been in a linear, traditional manner.

Thanks to the Arcturian teachings I came to understand that everything is energy, though of course nowadays scientists will assert that there's more it than that. However, for simplicity and ease it was a perfect way to see and come to understand how everything in our reality actually works. Clairvoyantly I saw the energy grid that not only surrounds all living things but came to realize that the whole human body exists within this life-enhancing energy grid. Without it there is nothing. I observed the energy grid, or matrix, as it was called in the Keanu Reeves movie, The Matrix.

It was obvious that this energy grid is often damaged in the human body. I saw it as fractured, blocked, weakened, distorted and more. When working with clients it's this energy grid that I worked to correct.

Once corrected then the physical body began to heal on many levels. Of course, sometimes it would take a few sessions for this to happen, other times the energy corrections resulted in almost immediate physical healing.

I also saw this matrix outside in the natural world and was able to correct misalignments and energy fractures that had occurred in nature. During this time of intense learning there were numerous, too many in fact to list, occasions where I observed and felt corrections take place.

One such occurrence took place in a large bay some distance away. I'd been guided to this area, without knowing why but had learned to trust my teachers implicitly by then. This area was completely unfamiliar; I'd never been there before. At the time I was in the company of three other people. Standing still I looked out across the bay, the expansive ocean was quite some distance away. Small waves rippled constantly across the bay even though there was little or no wind. Slowly energy began pouring down into my head and through my body, radiating out of both hands and feet. This lasted for quite some time and I remained absolutely still, completely clueless as to the why or whatever of the situation.

When the energy downpour ended I was startled to hear one of my companions say, "I've lived here over a quarter of a century. In all that time I've never seen the waves stop. The water in the bay is completely calm!" Looking up and out over the horizon I saw what he meant. There wasn't a wavelet in sight. The water was as smooth as silk. Without hesitation I told them about a weakness in the earth's crust some twenty-five kilometres south west from where we were standing. The energy that had been channelled via my body had corrected that weakness. How did I know this? I just did. It was not my first foray into strengthening the earth's crust. In fact, a great deal of time and energy had been expended in doing earth healing over the years. My role was merely that of being a conduit. Around the world there were plenty of other people doing similar work.

"The day science begins to study non-physical phenomena it will make more progress in one decade than in all the previous centuries of its existence."

Nikola Tesla

CHAPTER 12

Scientists studying quantum physics and quantum consciousness talk about wave form energy. Having seen and experienced this surreal event has been a real bonus. The first time it occurred was when I was behind the wheel of the car driving along the highway. Suddenly all I saw ahead was this massive energy field moving in wave form formation. It was literally impossible to see the road. Instead there was this energy matrix moving strongly yet gently in wave form right before my eyes. I felt myself and the car dissolve as I drove through it, and it remained that way for several seconds before normal visual acuity returned.

Was the experience spooky or eerie? Not at all. It was an amazing experience to have, one that was indescribable. Similar experiences occurred unexpectedly at different times. It was as though all that was physical completely dissolved or disappeared and all that existed was part of this enormous wave form formation that moves effortlessly and silently throughout creation.

Other energy experiences that opened my eyes to the reality of energy being the basis of everything also took place. One such situation occurred when I was lying on a massage table and spiritual healing took place. Spiritual healing is a non-contact modality where practitioners become a conduit for energy flow from the universe. It works on subtle levels and induces feelings of calm and healing within. Two or three really good friends were standing around the table, as we had arranged an afternoon of sharing and relaxing with this beautiful energy.

Suddenly there was a wave of strong energy pulsing through my body. Its intensity increased greatly in a very short space of time and before I knew it my body was levitating off the table. I felt this incredible cushioning effect beneath and all around, as though I were cocooned within an air bubble and my body was gently lifted upwards. Suddenly my mind went, "Wow, I'm levitating!" That conscious thought interfered with whatever was happening and with a thud my body dropped back onto the table surface. As well, several other incidents demonstrated clearly that everything is energy. At times I would lean back into a chair and would literally feel my body move through the solid back of the chair, and had to halt my backwards movement for fear that I would fall onto the floor. Incidents such as this happened, I believe, to shift my awareness and understanding of reality to a new level.

One incident in particular was not for public knowledge; it was kept secret for many years. A dear friend had arrived for an energy healing session. By this stage I no longer practised Reiki as the energy that was channelled through my hands was far more powerful. For some inexplicable reason I was standing by the side of the massage table, near where her head lay and suddenly there was a massive whoosh of energy. Within a nanosecond I found myself standing inside a large, gloomy room where only a lamp provided light. The room was stately, there were tall windows with long, heavy curtains that had been drawn back with tassels. I felt myself standing behind one the curtains observing whatever was transpiring in the room. There was a sizable desk, behind which stood a solid office chair. The desk was actually very large and impressive, obviously made of solid wood. Alongside the desk stood two men, both wearing old fashioned suits. One passed an envelope to the other. Softly spoken words were exchanged. Immediately I knew that the person passing the envelope, which contained a lot of money, was Vice-President Lyndon B. Johnson.

Without knowing how I knew, I knew that he was the person responsible for plotting and ensuring the carrying out of the assassination of John F Kennedy. All this information was immediately available in a fraction of a second. This event had happened in the nineteen sixties, yet I saw it all clearly. Somehow I'd managed to time travel. Then, just as suddenly I was catapulted back into my own space.

My friend asked, "What the hell happened? One minute you were here, then you weren't."

I told her what had occurred and asked that she tell no-one. She then described how I'd been fully present one moment and then suddenly I'd gone, even though my physical body remained standing. It was as though I'd gone into a trance state, possibly catatonic, and there was no way she could reach me. It was only many years later that I came across a lot of official de-classified information that confirmed what I'd seen. It all made perfect sense once I read a great deal more about witness testimony and other suppressed details.

To this day I know the reality of what had been seen and experienced. This particular incident prompted my interest in learning more about the actual truth of what takes place in the world. Stories told in the media are skewed in ways so as to become a parody of the real truth. That one particular incident showed clearly the duplicity and dishonesty existing in this world. It opened my eyes and resulted in an ongoing quest to find the truth, which often meant delving deeply beneath the layers of propaganda and manipulation occurring on many levels within our shared co-created reality.

∞∞∞∞∞

Often I attempted to make sense of the theories of quantum physics and consciousness. Internet research intensified and at times it became furious. Scientific articles were devoured. The science was complex, yet when explained in a simplified form was easier to understand and was very relatable to the energy healing work undertaken. In particular it made a great deal of sense when applied to the principles of channelling, where the energy of the person channelling and the spirit guides being channelled must resonate within a similar frequency range or band width. Incidents such as the ones shared above helped greatly in my understanding of its relevance and applicability.

Theory is one thing. Seeing the theory in action gave it credence and validity. Ultimately I came to understand the concepts of energy frequency, vibration, wave energy, energy grid, and more. In particular, it was heartening to read about the cosmic universe existing within this pulsing energy web or matrix, that it is part of everything and that we are part of it; that all consciousness exists within this framework. Whoever created this was a genius, but to know that it existed within each and every one of us completely confirmed what I'd always known. That energy called God exists within everything, including within every person. It's not an outside entity or force. Understanding this dynamic ended my differences with this thing called God, yet even to this day

I acknowledge the Creator or All That Is in preference to using the particular God word.

The Arcturus Community were my teachers for several years. It was through their constant guidance that opportunities for further understanding occurred. They were my constant companions and took every opportunity to extend my spiritual growth. A second book, never published, was channelled, again with the same intensity as the first. My trust in their guidance strengthened further. At one stage I found myself guided to my car at regular intervals. Once seated I was guided to drive. Instructions such as, "Turn left" followed by "Turn Right" would be heard in my head. Before I knew it I'd been guided along countless unfamiliar roads into places I'd never seen before. Sometimes the journeys were of considerable length. Yet always I would end up back in my own driveway. Maybe this experience was the precursor to what we now accept as commonplace satellite navigation!

The guided driving instructions were preparation for my next adventure. A three week trip to Nepal and India loomed on the agenda. The Arcturians were specific about this; it took place several weeks after 9/11. At that stage there was still great panic and fear around the safety of air travel. Regardless, I booked a ticket to land in Kathmandu and to depart from Calcutta. What would happen between arrival and departure dates hadn't been determined. All I knew was that there was a particular word, "Trust" that kept popping into my head. During this trip cryptic messages would pop into consciousness. These cryptic messages were meant to guide me throughout the trip. Figuring them out was a challenge and so I asked for a sign that my understanding was correct. The signs that cropped up time and again were either the appearance of an eagle overhead or a butterfly nearby.

In my luggage I'd brought pencils and other educational materials suitable for young children. I'd been tasked to donate them to a certain monastery in Nepal. In doing the research it seemed this was not such an easy task as there were monasteries all over the country. Eventually, using intuition I found a monastery that might have been the designated one. As I walked around the monastery gardens I was in appreciation of its beauty. Walking up a flight of garden steps I asked spirit guides to give some sign as to indicate that this was the correct monastery. The garden steps were uneven so my eyes were focused on the ground. In front of me suddenly there was a large butterfly sitting on the next step. It hadn't flown there. It hadn't been there before. It completely manifested out of nothing. That was my confirmation.

During this trip, which was undertaken one step at a time depending on the cryptic guidance of spirit guides I came to rely fully on living day to day and being open to all possibilities. I enjoyed rides on the back of small motor bikes, slept on benches in public bus depots, hiked in the Himalayas, spent time at Buddha's birthplace, volunteered at Mother Teresa's orphanage and more.

One of the most rewarding of all experiences was roaming the Himalayas where the Dalai Lama had set up his residence. I was stunned by the fast and reliable internet access everywhere I travelled. One particular conversation with a Buddhist nun in one of the many internet cafes remains with me to this day, only because it really jarred. Smiling broadly she said, "I hate computers". The energy in the word 'hate' was sufficient to send a jolt throughout my body. It was shocking to hear because it's a word that had disappeared fully from my vocabulary long before and it was the last word I'd expected to hear from a practicing devotee. The Arcturian teachings around the power of energy had attuned me to the vibration and frequency of language and its usage. Consequently quite a number of words had been eliminated from my thoughts and oral language due to their low, or dense, frequency.

No matter where I went there were magnificent eagles or butterflies to guide the way. I witnessed poverty and suffering to a degree that was totally unfamiliar, and which should have been gross or untenable. Yet the indomitable spirit in the people was inspiring. No matter the hardship everywhere I saw peace and compassion within the faces. There was no evidence of ADHD, anxiety, depression or many of the normal stresses manifested in our western culture. It seemed as though there was faith or compassion that radiated from within. I was greatly struck by and impressed with the spirit of the people, and knew that inner peace and acceptance were part of what was woven into the fabric of this culture. Whatever it was that produced this energy of inner peace and equanimity I knew that it was worth aspiring to, that I would devote time and energy to developing it within.

It was no accident that I'd been guided to Nepal and India. Intuition and trust in the unseen had been strengthened to an unbelievable degree. Experiencing a totally foreign culture, and doing it without staying at three or more star accommodation, had been a humbling experience. I fell in love with the culture, food and the people. Along with this I felt the stirrings of compassion to a degree not previously experienced or understood. Judgment and negative thinking had no place in my life, given the abundance and the benefits I'd received throughout my life.

∞∞∞∞

Psychics are expected to be able to predict what is still to unfold in someone's life, and often this can be done with a high degree of accuracy. Unfortunately, in most instances, psychics are unable to see into their own future. They generally lack this ability, and it can be cause of great frustration. Initially upon discovering that I possessed some psychic abilities it was with great enthusiasm that I undertook the onerous task of attempting to unravel what was yet to happen in my life. Surprisingly my success rate was reasonably high. Somehow I had the knack of investigative exploration, which enabled glimpses of what would occur next and even in the future. Not satisfied with this I also began investigations into other lifetimes.

In some ways this was truly about understanding myself better. I'd spent a large part of my life conforming to others' expectations and in the process had diminished or even annihilated my sense of self to the extent that I'd ended up not knowing who I was. Figuring out both other lifetimes and potential future outcomes seemed one way of assisting in formulating a sense of identity.

A great deal of this investigative work occurred during times of mental dialogue with spirit guides. It was simply a matter of asking the right questions or sometimes asking countless questions in the hope of gaining some titbit of information. Building up a relationship where there was ongoing dialogue had taken time, but by then I'd become comfortable with the patterns of speech and the responses given. Often I'd hear the word 'trust' and gradually trust in dialogue had developed. One day in the midst of some serious questioning I heard this statement, "It is not necessary to know everything in advance. Allow us to surprise you."

One of the advantages of this kind of communication is that often it's not the words themselves but the instantaneous knowing that occurs from time to time. The knowing this time was that I clairvoyantly saw large parcels gift wrapped and with bows. This told me that the element of surprise could be valuable and enjoyable. After hearing that statement I stopped the pestering and began focusing more predominantly on living in the moment.

That didn't mean my knowing of what was to happen was stopped. Instead it still occurred when it was meant to. One such knowing, shared with close friends, was that one day a tall, handsome man would come to my practice and he would be the love of my life. Not long after sharing this information the man turned up and turned my life upside down. During our first date we shared our hopes and aspirations. As I opened up about my personal journey and where I saw it going he asked, "Where do I fit into this?"

"I don't know," was my response.

Intuitively I knew that he didn't, just as I knew then that this relationship would not be long term. Despite knowing this I was determined to enjoy it for as long as was possible. I was fortunate and deeply grateful to have known him and to feel such deep soul love, even while knowing that nothing else in future would match up to the depth of this connection.

Some years earlier I'd had the awareness that I would be travelling to the States. When the awareness or knowing comes in it often feels as though it comes from far left field and sometimes I'm not ready or am unwilling to entertain the potential that is presented. I definitely had no desire or interest in ever visiting the States, so that particular knowing was effortlessly relegated to the back of the cupboard to be forgotten immediately. Not long after this another knowing emerged that I'd be going to the United Kingdom. This particular knowing held a lot of appeal and immediately I began saving for an extended trip. Ultimately that plan bombed at that stage, mainly because it wasn't the right time for it to happen.

Having some knowing of what lies ahead can be both a bonus and an annoyance. I'd purchased a home and taken great joy in doing home improvements. My mind wandered in all sorts of creative ways to really make this home something special. With a budget in mind it was feasible, providing I undertook renovation projects one at a time over a gradual and possibly lengthy period of time. Immersing myself in creative energy was inspiring and exciting. The only dampener occurred not long after I'd moved in when I heard spirit guides alert me to the fact that this would not be my home for long. Their suggestion that I undertake minimal improvements reduced my innovative drive greatly.

"As long as you have certain desires about how it ought to be you can't see how it is."

Ram Dass

CHAPTER 13

Everything was going extremely well. For the first time in my life it actually felt as if there was a comfortable flow and ease. There was plenty of laughter, fun and enjoyment that provided a harmonious balance to the more serious side of my personality. The desire to continually explore and learn was always deep within, yet the widening circle of friends and the feelings of satisfaction around having made this massive transition into a new life brought about an inner peace that had been absent for most of my life. My relationship with my youngest son, while still fragile and brittle at times was still evolving. It was far from ideal but we were on speaking terms and I took every opportunity to spend time with him and to assure him of my love and continued role in his life. I had reconciled to the fact that this might take many years to be fully healed though remained optimistic about eventually developing a positive and loving relationship.

Little did I know that my exceptionally comfortable and enjoyable life was about to come to a shuddering end. My time with the Arcturians was winding down. The intense learning was easing and in my ignorance I'd overlooked an important piece of information that spirit had provided during the early stages of my spiritual awakening. It went along these lines. We all have what is referred to as the Book of Lives. For some individuals a lifetime may contain very little information in their book prior to incarnating, and their book would be filled as they went along. Instead I'd been told, "Your Book of Life for this lifetime is completely full. We will do all that is possible to ensure you do not disappoint yourself. We will push hard if that is what is needed. We would not wish for you to be disappointed."

Unexpectedly I kept getting a strong sense that it was time to go to the States. Consciously I had no interest or intention. Yet this message continued and intensified. My response was, "It's not possible. I don't have the money, and I can't leave what I've created here." Oh, I had every plausible excuse to ignore the inner knowing. On some level I was loath to leave everything I'd worked so hard to create. Even my strong desire for adventure had disappeared. I was in a real comfort zone and wasn't about to have it disturbed regardless of whatever my spirit guides might insist needed to happen.

That was probably the only time I've ever ignored the inner knowing or the quiet voice that whispered in my ears. Digging my heels in felt good. Nothing and no-one was going to shift me out of this space. One day a dear friend called. "I've got a message for you," Libby said, "You'd better sit down."

"Okay."

Libby continued, "My house is filled with spirit. They're all talking and they want you to listen. You are to go to the States."

"Easy said," was my response "but I don't have the ready cash that this trip would cost."

"Yes you do, and you know what you have to do. Spirit has already told you. Sell your house."

"Well, yes, they've told me three times but I ignored what they said because I just don't want to do that," was my stubborn response.

"You're meant to go. Don't procrastinate, and remember I'm only the messenger," was her parting comment.

That night I grumbled for hours and mentally railed against the fates. Every possible reason for not going ran through my mind and was dissected in great detail. On another level I knew deep down that this edict could not be ignored – unfortunately! I'd amply demonstrated my trust in spirit just as they'd reciprocated with love and respect. My life had been enriched beyond belief due to their presence and guidance. They accepted my human weaknesses, guided with understanding whenever I faltered or failed to live up to my own expectations. Everything they'd delivered had been delivered with unconditional love. Maybe, just maybe, there were reasons unknown to me that this trip needed to happen. The least I could do was investigate just what was involved. It wouldn't hurt to go through the motions, and if things didn't work out then I could claim that at least I'd made an effort.

Co-incidentally I'd arranged to meet another friend for coffee early the next morning. Once we were seated I explained my dilemma.

His immediate response was, "I have a friend who works in the real estate office a few doors down. Let's go see him about getting a house appraisal." The appraisal was carried out within a few days. Some minor cosmetic improvements were suggested to enhance the appearance of the house, which didn't take long to complete. In the meantime I made enquiries about gaining a twelve month visitor visa to the States, airline travel and more.

The whole process was effortless. I gave myself seven weeks in which to have everything completed. The house sold on the first weekend it was open to viewing and the sale transaction processed smoothly. Visitor visa was granted. Car sold. Household furniture was donated to charities and the remaining personal possessions were placed in storage. Within five weeks everything was arranged and completed. My home was no longer mine. If it hadn't been for the generosity of another friend who offered the use of a spare bedroom for the remaining two weeks I would have been living on the streets. Those two remaining weeks were spent socializing and partying. I'd decided it was an opportunity to spend time with the many beautiful friends made in the few years I'd lived in this city. Those two weeks passed in a whirlwind of shared laughter and fun.

Initially as the process of de-constructing my life commenced my stress levels skyrocketed. Libby, ever the wise woman, sat me down and provided sage advice, advice that I've shared with countless other people since that time. "You're panicking because all you can see is the mountain of work that's involved in making this happen. Stop focusing on the whole picture. Instead figure out what your next step is and make that your priority. As you begin nearing the end of that particular step then begin figuring out what the following step after that just happens to be. Before you know it you'll have all the steps completed and you'll have finished everything without stressing yourself out to the max."

Those wise and simple words of strategy planning and organizing made all the difference to my mental outlook, helping calm nerves and greatly reducing any worries. During this time I also learned a powerful lesson. When something is meant to be then the universe makes sure it happens. The ease and speed with which this whole process of de-constructing my life occurred was surprising and often overwhelming. I felt as though I was in a meditative zone, nothing was too difficult or challenging. There were no impediments to the process. The flow was unstoppable. Obviously I was meant to travel to the States. When asked, time and again, "What are you going to be doing once you arrive in the States?" I had to admit that I had no idea. My only plan of action was to see what happened and follow my intuition and guidance, in much the same way as had happened when I'd travelled through Nepal and India less than twelve months earlier.

Regardless of the speed and ease of winding down my life there were countless moments of reflection and questioning. What was going to happen? Would I be safe? How would I survive? Why did I have to leave everything behind? Most of all were the recollections of the happy times spent in my house and the highly enjoyable lifestyle that had been created. Having seen myself as being an outsider for most of my life I really felt as though I'd found a haven, or niche, in this place.

Being accepted by others was a new experience, one that I'd given up hope of ever happening. It had been an eye opener finding that there were people like myself, whose thinking was more lateral and off tangent, who didn't judge or criticize. Best of all was that out in the wider world there were people who questioned the *status quo*, who looked deeper into things and who were also finding comfort in marching to the beat of their own uniqueness. These beautiful souls often had had similar background experiences; they were often the odd one in their family of birth, the one person whose ideas, ideology and beliefs were in contrast to family teachings. It was especially difficult to leave; having finally found a circle of friends that had become my soul family I had no desire to start my life anew.

∞∞∞∞

Jet lagged and weary I looked out at the lights of Los Angeles as the plane neared the airport preparing for descent. All I saw was a sprawling metropolis, lights glinting far and wide and a layer of smoggy pollution over it. "Let the adventures begin," was my first thought. The first two days were spent exploring Santa Monica and Venice Beach areas. It was the middle of summer and holiday festivities were in the air. Yet for some reason it didn't feel right to remain there too long. It was strange being in a foreign country, not knowing a soul and with no program or routine to follow. This could easily have been a long awaited vacation but as it had been a long time since I'd had a proper vacation my mind wasn't in the space to even contemplate relaxing for a few days.

Instead, I looked for transport to take me out of Los Angeles and immediately found a coach trip up the west coast along Highway 1. It took two days to arrive in San Francisco, with frequent stops along the way to enjoy the touristy sights. Once ensconced in San Francisco it was apparent that if I was to travel anywhere in the States then a set of wheels would be needed. A full day spent walking up and down a used car strip in the hot afternoon sun eventually resulted in the purchase of a blue coupe, which had seen better days but still had plenty of mileage left. Armed with countless maps of California, picked up from the national automotive association office, I headed out full of bravado and with no idea of direction or destination.

"What was I thinking?" I asked myself again and again. "I don't know a soul. Don't know where to go or what to do! Why did I even embark upon this pointless exercise?" By this stage I'd driven on the Interstate highway, with nerves on edge, teeth chattering and hands clenched tightly on the steering wheel. It was murder on the multiple laned highways, with vehicles zipping in and out effortlessly and all I could do was hope that I didn't end up killing myself or anyone. These roads had five or six lanes filled with traffic heading in the one direction, which was a totally new and terrifying driving experience. Added to this stress was the fact that I'd never driven on the right side of the road before, which certainly presented quite a novel learning opportunity.

Traffic moved fast, certainly faster than I would have liked. All I could do was hang on tightly and trust that I was in the right lane, and would be able to read the street exit signs as they loomed ahead in the distance. Everything was in a whirl and it wasn't long before I was talking to my guides, to the gods or to anyone who was listening and who could help steer me in the right direction. My first experiences driving on the right side of the road were without doubt quite challenging and nerve racking. Yet I survived. The maps I'd collected were easy to follow and somehow day after day I managed to find my way around the state.

Before I knew it I'd been in California a whole month. A month spent driving and exploring. With some trepidation I'd managed to drive successfully and safely through the manic traffic in San Francisco, Los Angeles and other cities. Each day brought new journeys and scenery. As had been my habit when travelling in Nepal and India I trusted in my guidance. Each morning, upon waking I'd check the maps and mentally ask, "Where to, today?" and somehow I knew. In many of the places visited energy work was undertaken on the earth. In other places I found an opportunity to enjoy the majestic views, breathe in fresh air, enjoy nature's abundant energies and more. However, by the end of that first month I was feeling very lonely and isolated. Phone calls back to friends in Australia eased the loneliness pangs only briefly. I was roaming idly and felt directionless. More importantly I was also feeling forgotten by my spirit guides. Not once had I been able to get a glimpse of what was to come or what I needed to do. Instead the days rolled one into the next and the aimlessness had begun to take a toll.

In a fit of frustration I figured that most of California had been explored, especially most the scenic sights and major tourist destinations of interest, and it was possibly time to challenge myself by venturing further. It was time to drive across the Mojave Desert. I'd heard about it, about the Interstate highway that wove across the parched, desolate landscape. By this time I'd become fully versed with all the information provided in the thick Lonely Planet guidebook. The South West looked interesting and definitely vastly different to the densely populated state of California.

Needless to say the drive across the desert felt never ending. Hot sun beat down. The landscape was arid and looked hostile. My mind wandered, thinking of all the stories I'd read about this desert and the Native American tribes that had lived in the area. There was definitely a certain vibe to the land that was palpable and evident every time I stopped to take in yet another vista. During this drive my thoughts were on aloneness, solitude, the nature of being human, surviving against all odds and other oddball topics. Having left behind such a rich and diverse community in Australia I was confronting myself, analysing motivations, perceptions, beliefs and actions. There were no distractions at all, just me and my out of control mind for company. And that was not necessarily a positive experience.

Eventually the desert was left behind and I neared Flagstaff, Arizona. It was late on a Friday afternoon. My intention was to spend the night there but upon driving through the outer parts of town wasn't feeling a strong positive vibe and decided to continue on to Sedona. Unexpectedly a massive and violent storm broke out. Lightning, thunder and extremely heavy rain downpour forced a stop. Visibility had become virtually impossible. Immediately ahead was a motel so I pulled in, planning to stay just the one night providing the storm was only brief and would clear overnight.

"You're lucky, there's only one room left," the clerk at the motel informed me.

"Really, why is it so busy?"

"It's Labor Day weekend. Plus there's a Hells' Angels convention happening here this weekend."

I looked out the window. By this time the rain had eased and people were once again out and about. I didn't see a single motorbike or any sign of people with leather jackets, tattoos or helmets. The clerk continued, "If you look closely you'll see FBI agents everywhere in town. They're here keeping an eye on things, to make sure that everyone behaves. You'll definitely see the Hells Angels people everywhere over the next few days. Just make sure you stay out of their way and you'll be fine."

I asked about the sudden storm and downpour. "Oh, it's monsoon season, it rains like this most days during the month but it doesn't last for long."

After deciding to stay for longer than one night due to the fact that it would have been difficult finding motel accommodation in Sedona or elsewhere on the Labor Day weekend I went outside, deciding to explore the town. The torrential rain had completely stopped and the sun was shining brightly. As I walked along the footpaths I didn't immediately see any signs of the Hells Angels until I turned a corner and was met by quite a large number of them. Remembering the friendly advice handed out by the clerk I kept my eyes down, averted them and moved quickly. Little did I know then that in time I'd end up becoming friendly with the president of the local Hells Angels chapter, meet his family and support him through a journey with cancer.

My intention to stay only for a weekend proved to be wishful thinking. Instead I remained in Flagstaff for two years. During this time I travelled extensively throughout the state along with visiting other states in the south west, and came to love its unique energy, its wildness, history and the hodgepodge of characters whose paths intersected with mine.

"Experience is a hard teacher, because she gives the test first, the lesson afterward."

Vernon Law

CHAPTER 14

One of my biggest concerns about spending time in the States was whether or not it would be possible to meet like-minded souls, or whether I would once again feel like a square peg in a round hole. Having enjoyed the companionship and friendship of other individuals whose life outlook was similar to mine I no longer had any inclination or desire to revert back to being the outsider, the one who had difficulty conforming to expectations or standards that didn't resonate in the slightest. Realistically though I was somewhat optimistic due to the fact that the population in the States is large, and a lot of the books I'd read on spirituality, metaphysics and the paranormal had been published in the States. Ultimately it came down to that particular word, the one I'd heard too often but which had proved itself again and again – Trust!

Almost immediately I was made to feel welcome. Meeting people became effortless; obviously the universe, or my spirit guides, had it all planned out. I just hadn't been told about the schedule in advance. No matter where I went I met individuals who in time would end up becoming good friends. Instead of staying in bare, unappealing motel rooms I spent long periods of time in family homes with delightful people as hosts. The generosity of spirit and kindness shown was surprising and humbling. In exchange for a bed and use of facilities I gifted my healing abilities, and shared the channelled wisdom that I'd been privy to. It was considered a fair exchange of energy yet I always knew that my receiving was greater than what I gave.

Once accepted into the metaphysical community it was surprising just how many new introductions were made. Sedona was about an hour's drive from Flagstaff and while I had anticipated that I would spend a lot of time there it didn't actually happen. The town of Sedona, to my mind, was little more than a tourist trap despite all the great things I'd read about it previously. The real magic was to be found in the surrounding natural scenery. Sedona is known for the powerful energy vortices, the high frequency spots found in the nearby hills and red rocks. There is no doubt that the vortices exist.

The highlight of my few visits to Sedona occurred when a delightful elderly shaman suggested that we spend a day hiking the trails in the area. He assured me that he knew the area well and that he would show me some of the power spots. That trip was eventful, not because of any magical or spiritual experience, but because of two things. The first was that an unexpected and lengthy monsoonal downpour occurred, with loud thunder and lightning flashing extremely close by. We were walking along high ridges and at times the lightning flashes were almost too close for comfort. Instead of feeling fear I felt euphoric and energized by the raw magic and power of Mother Nature. In practically no time at all we were both fully drenched. I couldn't stop laughing, the feeling of being truly alive was intense and every minute spent in this wild weather was a tonic for the soul. The second reason the trip was eventful is that my shaman friend managed to get us lost. His innate direction radar let us down badly and by the time we eventually stumbled back to his car we both looked bedraggled, saturated and the worse for wear. A short drive later we found a delightful Mexican café where, over a delicious meal, we agreed wholeheartedly that the day had been both eventful and unforgettable.

In Tucson where I also spent quite a bit of time I had the good fortune to meet other like-minded souls. One incident stands out clearly, not because it was positive but because it brought to the surface deep seated fears of extreme fright and helplessness. From a very early age I'd had a thing about uniforms and what they represent. Every time I saw a police officer my breath would become shallow, my body rigid and my danger antenna would be on high alert. Even having a police vehicle behind me in traffic was sufficient to trigger this response. A recurring dream over many years was about avoiding men in uniform, hiding from them under the cover of darkness. Just seeing that uniform or any representation of its authority was sufficient to set my teeth on edge. This fear, obviously, was not one that I'd overcome when working through the countless exercises and strategies recommended in the book *Feel the Fear and Do It Anyway*.

I'd been staying with a lovely couple, and through them had met countless other interesting individuals. These encounters were extremely helpful as they aided my understanding of the lifestyle and psyche of the American people. I was rapidly coming to realize that while there were similarities with the Australian ethos there were definitely differences. Overall however the generosity and kindness experienced was beyond belief. One morning the lady of this particular residence where I was staying for only a short period of time woke me up early, asking if I'd be able to help out as there was an emergency. Her husband had taken their only car and wouldn't be home for some time. She had received a phone call from a friend requesting her help urgently.

Once in my car the whole story poured out. Apparently my passenger had been asked to come and pick up two young children and to care for them for the time being. Their parents were being arrested and there was no one else to help out. All that I was asked to do was to be the designated driver. Following verbal directions we eventually pulled up outside a property. Upon seeing the scene outside the property my heart skipped a beat and my breath tightened. The place was filled with all kinds of military style police vehicles and there were plenty of fully armed police in sight. Immediately I knew this was a SWAT raid and if it had been possible would have turned around and fled. Luckily common sense prevailed and I pulled in slowly. Immediately two police officers walked up to the car, and my knees began shaking uncontrollably.

"What is your purpose in being here?"

My passenger got out of the car, informed them that she had come in response to a phone call and was going to pick up two young children. A nod of assent was given and an arm waved to indicate that she should go into the building. Meanwhile I sat there quaking in my seat, staring straight ahead and wishing the earth would swallow me whole. Next thing I heard and felt a hand rap on my car window and was asked to step out of the car. Acting as normal as possible I complied with that command. Then the questioning began.

"Do you have identification?"

I handed over my passport.

"Do you have identification or proof of ownership of the vehicle?"

"Yes," and I scrambled into the car to retrieve the relevant documents from the glovebox. Both officers looked everything over. One went to another vehicle and obviously checked out the validity of my papers.

"What are you doing here?" was the next question.

"I'm travelling around the States on a twelve month visitor visa. Along the way I meet different people, sometimes I stay with them for a while before moving on. This is a sabbatical for me. I'm taking time to experience something different."

The questioning continued, "Why did you drive here today?"

"I'm a guest at that lady's house for a few days. She asked if I'd drive her here to pick up the children. My car was the only one available and obviously I couldn't refuse. I used to be a teacher and know it's important that children be cared for, no matter what the situation or circumstances."

By this stage I was rattled and talking far too much. Mentally telling myself to zip the lips wasn't working. Nervousness and discomfort coursed throughout every cell in my body. The second officer came back with my passport and papers, and handed them to me.

"Thank you, your papers all check out."

With that they walked away. I got back into my car and waited, and waited. Eventually my passenger came out of the house accompanied by two police officers, one holding her by one of her arms. Both arms were behind her back, handcuffed. Seeing this I was flummoxed, stunned beyond words. She was then led to another police vehicle where she was guided into the back seat. There was no sign of the two children that we'd come to collect. I was in a quandary. Would it be safe to leave the scene? Or, was there still more that the police might want to ask?

This time my wait wasn't as lengthy. Another knock on the window and an officer spoke.

"Your friend has an outstanding warrant from out of state and is being detained for that purpose. It's unfortunate you have found yourself in this situation. This is not something you should have witnessed. Leave now and forget the whole thing. I wish you a relaxing and enjoyable time for the remainder of your time in the States."

Hands shaking I started the car and got out of there as quickly as possible. After finding my way back to her home I spoke with her partner, explained the situation, packed my stuff and drove out of the city. My response was one of sheer panic and the urge to flee out of all proportion to the experience or situation.

∞∞∞∞

Prior to leaving for the States I'd clairvoyantly seen an image of a man with silver hair, wearing a check shirt and jeans. This image had flitted into mind quite frequently before my departure. While I was curious about what this might mean I definitely didn't intend flying to the States to just meet someone, nor did I intentionally go looking for anyone. Instead, I was enjoying most of the encounters experienced along the way, with only the one obvious exception! However, I eventually met him at a social breakfast gathering and when our eyes connected a jolt of recognition flowed through my body. Immediately my mind went into overdrive. What was this about? Did we know one another from another lifetime? Did it mean anything? Did he pick up on it or was it merely my imagination?

I was a stranger in a strange country; my aloneness still accompanied me no matter where I went. Having no fixed abode and living out of suitcases was becoming old very rapidly. So by that stage a little romance wouldn't have gone astray or been unwelcome. My understanding of soul connection was that often there would be a spark of recognition, a feeling of soul knowing that might go beyond this lifetime. That recognition didn't necessarily mean it was romantic or sexual in nature, even though it might often be mistaken for that.

After that initial meeting we met up a few times and a friendship was gradually forged. We had a great deal in common and gradually that friendship turned into something more. Allan became my second husband, and we were blessed with a beautiful, simple marriage ceremony at the Grand Canyon.

The one thing missing from my life at that stage was a sense of career fulfilment. By this time I was well versed in understanding my own foibles and needs. One of those needs was to be gainfully employed in some way. I thoroughly enjoyed doing energy work, channelling and working with people. I'd undergone Reiki Master training some years earlier and was keen to teach others about the power of natural, vibrational healing. In Australia I'd conducted Reiki classes successfully and had found the experience both rewarding and fulfilling. Yet in the States I felt challenged as to how best to utilize my knowledge and skills. Somehow what should have been a simple problem to resolve actually felt complex and extremely challenging. The flow, as I'd experienced previously, just wasn't occurring in Arizona.

Population clusters are interesting to observe and understand. Overall the state of Arizona wasn't wealthy. There seemed to be few industries or wealth generating businesses. There was more of a redneck energy right across the state, though to make such a blanket statement would be erroneous. There was character, strength and adaptability within the population. Yet I intuitively knew that setting up a business in Arizona would be tough and it would take years of hard work to achieve anything, and I didn't have either the patience or time.

During this time I was fortunate to meet a few individuals, some of whom I'd describe as real characters. One of these was Len, president of the local chapter of Hells Angels. Len had been diagnosed with cancer and the medical prognosis wasn't promising. In time I came to see and understand the soft person that lay beneath the tough exterior. Len made exquisite jewellery and had crafted a spectacular necklace and matching earrings as a gift and which I valued and wore on special occasions. Len knew he was not going to be blessed with longevity and was seeking to transition to the other side in peace. He had many questions, he came for Reiki sessions and we talked for many hours about what was happening and what he could expect during this time of gradual transition. I felt fully qualified to support him through this journey as I'd completed an intensive hospice and palliative care training course, in addition to undertaking a lot of reading and research on the topic of death, dying and the afterlife. As well, Allan was a practising Buddhist when we met and in the course of our general and regular conversation we would cover all sorts of interesting concepts such as death, the dying and grieving process and more.

Len was fortunate in that he had a solid community of support. There was no doubt his Hells' Angels family was large and caring. However, he frequently sought out my company, especially as the ending neared, where it was evident that he was coming to terms with the finality of his illness, but even better he was finding peace within for the first time in his life. For that he thanked me, as it was through our shared conversations that he was able to let go of resentment, stored emotional pain and then come to some understanding of his life and its meaning. Towards the very end he showed compassion for all that he was experiencing, there was no sign of regret, resentment or bitterness. His passing was peaceful and he was surrounded by loved ones. Allan and I attended his funeral service and wake. We were the only white collar attendees, being only somewhat comfortable in the company of an enormous gathering of Hells Angels membe

"We change the world not by what we say or do, but as a consequence of what we have become."

Dr David Hawkins

CHAPTER 15

After days and weeks of discussion and exploring possibilities it was decided that a move to the Pacific North West would be a viable option. Allan was able to find employment and I intuitively knew that there would be ample opportunities for creating self-employment in the area. The Pacific North West was bustling with successful industries, was densely populated and also was considered to be progressive rather than conservative. At this stage of my life I was still adjusting to marriage, though often I questioned my sanity in once again entering into that particular partnership. The need to continually communicate, share and make allowances was at times extremely frustrating.

I'd lived alone comfortably, enjoyed communicating with spirit guides and following the inner dictates of intuition so the adjustments into relationship sharing were often challenging. Nevertheless, my spirit guides at the time had indicated that this was meant to be, and by this stage I'd learned that resistance was pointless. Ultimately I realized the validity of this guidance. In marrying a United States citizen I was then entitled to, and granted, a Green Card. At that particular time, however, such thoughts were far from mind as my focus was only on setting up and creating a natural therapies healing practice.

Having enjoyed working independently, teaching adults and all the associated variables of working in a field that was both exciting and different there was no doubt my soul craved more of this. The likelihood of becoming a stay at home wife, performing wifely duties such as shopping, cooking and cleaning were negligible, if not downright ridiculous. I craved a continuation of what had been commenced in Australia and my inner intuition and knowing was strong that the Pacific North West would be an ideal location for further learning and career opportunities.

The next phase of my spiritual learning and growth soon commenced. By this stage I'd become adept at finding businesses and people in any new area. Once located I would introduce myself, ask questions and from there commence the process of doing whatever felt appropriate to developing a healthy and enjoyable business practice. My initial search would be along these lines. Firstly find the organic health food stores as these generally host bulletin boards where practitioners and other related businesses in the health industry would advertise. Armed with information from the health food stores it was then a matter of visiting metaphysical bookstores and natural therapies clinics. Each visit would either generate interest from the business owner and would often provide additional possible contacts. It was basically a matter of putting together a mind map of contacts, opportunities and potentials.

Once the information had been garnered then it was time to make approaches to different business owners where I would deliver my sales pitch. What was I able to offer? How might it be compatible with their business model? Were our respective energies in alignment? Ironically, most of the joint decisions made were not based on logistics but more on the subtle energies, or vibes, that were a good match. Doing business in the metaphysical world was vastly different to undertaking business arrangements or deals in the regular three dimensional world reality.

It's never easy starting over. Having to prove myself once again was tedious, yet I knew that it was important to create a positive impression and to meld into the larger groups of natural therapies and metaphysical practitioners. At the first holistic expo I attended a successful astrologer in the area said, "It takes three years for anyone new to the area to be fully accepted by the public." His words were meant to reassure me that it would take both time and patience. I wasn't reassured in the least. Having left behind a practice that I'd built up steadily, the idea of starting over again from scratch held absolutely no appeal. Sometimes all that's needed to provide the impetus to make haste is something as simple as his statement. My determination to prove that it was possible to build up a reputable career and earning income was fuelled by a desire to find and use every potential opportunity along the way. I was on a mission and nothing was going to stop me.

∞∞∞∞

One thing that had been missing in my journey, or so I believed, was a wise and long term teacher. It's commonplace in spiritual circles for students to find a master, someone who has already undertaken many years of study and meditation prior to attaining wisdom, and who then shares that wisdom with the keen student. There is a common saying, "When the student is ready, the teacher appears". I had been ready for a number of years and was intent on finding my long term teacher. My teacher would be a Native American Indian and would be waiting for my arrival in the States. That was my belief and it I intended making it become a reality.

While living in Arizona and exploring the South West my determination to find the right teacher knew no bounds. I spent time with an Apache tribal member. He gifted me a handmade 'speaking' stick. When seated in a communal circle the person holding that stick was entitled to speak. Upon receipt of that gift I felt a strong vibration pouring through my hands. That vibration strengthened and increased. My eyes blinked and clairvoyantly I saw the room fill with Native American chiefs of All Nations. Their energy was strong. My Apache host and others in the room also saw the same thing happening. Messages were given. The room hummed with powerful vibes. My body responded to the strong vibration until gradually the vision faded, leaving us feeling replete and blessed.

More than once I drove up to the Navajo and Hopi Indian reservations with the hope of connecting meaningfully with tribal tribe members. I had the good fortune to find remnants from an Anasazi tribe encampment. The story I'd heard was that the tribe had inexplicably and completely disappeared from Arizona. Despite this I could still feel their energy in certain areas. Possibly their spirits still roamed across their homeland. I never could be quite sure but whenever I ventured into certain places I definitely felt their presence.

Like many others seeking a deeper meaning to life I truly believed that the serious answers could only be found outside of myself. I believed that my knowing was small and had to be enriched from another's fount of knowledge. When the opportunity arose to do a sweat lodge in the Pacific North West my excitement reached fever pitch. This might just be the beginning of what I had been searching for. Undertaking the sweat lodge experience indicates seriousness of intention, and preparation for one is necessary. Allan and I were eager for the experience. We turned up at the venue after driving some miles to find it and after having followed obscure directions. There was a motley group of serious and intent looking participants waiting. We prepared, following the instructions provided. We were told that there would be four parts to the sweat lodge, what was entailed in each part and that there would be an opportunity between parts to leave the sweat lodge for a short bathroom break or drink of water if needed.

Slowly I moved into the sweat lodge and squeezed into a spot near the back. It was cramped and still more people were entering. The body heat added to the inside temperature though I was aware that the first quarter wouldn't be too intensely hot. However, no sooner had I begun to relax when a loud voice screamed in my ears, "Get out!" I kept hearing those two words repeated over a period of several minutes. It just wasn't possible. The space was filled with people, many of whom were going into a meditative space. To disturb them would have been disrespectful. Finally I mentally responded, "I can't move yet but will do so as soon as there is a break in proceedings." With that commitment made I spent the remainder of the first quarter of the sweat lodge sitting upright with my eyes wide open and mind fully alert. As soon as possible I stumbled outside and didn't return.

To this day I still am not sure what would have happened if I'd remained and completed the sweat lodge. My trust lay with that voice inside my head. It had never let me down and never would. Obviously I didn't need a teacher or master when the voice or voices had regularly demonstrated this capability clearly. It was only ego mind that felt the need to look up to someone else's teachings for guidance. After this experience I stopped searching for a teacher or master.

On reflection, Daisy had taught me well and her wisdom had provided guidance for many years. In reality all the knowledge ever needed actually lies within; it's always there for each and every person. It's a matter of having trust in the process of remembering what has been forgotten. The soul is all knowing and has access to universal consciousness. Upon incarnating into a lifetime that knowledge is fully there and it's only as we grow and adjust to human life that gradually memory of that knowledge disappears. Upon awakening once again into consciousness of true reality, and stepping out of the human illusion, that is when the master within emerges.

∞∞∞∞

It was surprisingly easy to adjust to a new life in the Pacific North West after this reminder about the power that lay within each human being. Once again I experienced an amazing amount of ease and speed in accomplishing the changes needed to become established as a practitioner in the area. It obviously was meant to be. Soon I attended classes, learning material and skills that had not been readily available in Australia. My time refraining from reading books and attending classes was over. There was no message received saying that my tenure as a student of the Arcturian teachings was over. Tentatively I sensed that our unwritten contract had come to an end and was willing to explore other avenues for further learning if needed. Nevertheless, I was surprisingly discerning about any selections made to increase knowledge, skills and understanding. I had been blessed with having the Arcturians as spirit guides; their teachings had been invaluable and would remain embedded within. They had provided a comprehensive education on the nature and power of energy, during which time I'd experienced some incredible mind blowing altered states involving universal cosmic energy. As a result my trust in the voices, my intuition and discernment ability had increased dramatically.

My understanding and knowledge of the human energy body along with experiences of the wider cosmic energy matrix would provide the basis for the work that was to follow. Before too long I was working out of several metaphysical outlets, seeing clients on a one on one basis, writing articles for magazines, channelling for clients, participating in holistic expos in addition to finding myself becoming part of a large and supportive natural therapies practitioner network. While it seemed effortless there is no doubt that a great deal of energy was expended in creating this diverse and interesting self-employed lifestyle.

∞∞∞∞

Of particular interest were the incredible healthy eating options available in the States. Maintaining a vegetarian lifestyle for over twenty years had been somewhat of a challenge when living in Australia. Nevertheless creativity and imagination had resulted in a relatively varied diet over the years. Some years earlier I'd begun doing regular cleanses and had become especially fussy about purchasing produce from reputable growers. Time was often spent searching out roadside stalls, going to markets in order to purchase chemical free produce. Upon arriving in the Pacific North West I quickly discovered large organic food stores and was convinced I'd arrived in a gourmet's heaven.

Those intense energy zapping sessions where electrical like currents had flowed through my body for periods of time had convinced me of the importance of being clean on all levels. The physical body, I'd come to understand, is a temple that houses the soul and it had become important to treat it with the utmost care and respect. In order to maintain a healthy body only the cleanest, healthiest foods would suffice. Clean living became my mantra long before it was recognized and adopted by the wider public. Even at this stage my adherence to such a lifestyle was generally perceived as being a bit "over the top" by colleagues and friends alike.

My Arcturian guides had stressed the importance of holding a frequency sufficiently high in order to be able to create an energy resonance match. Those earlier energy zapping sessions had divested me of a great deal of energy and cellular pain memories on the emotional and mental levels. It was my responsibility to keep my physical body in a strong, healthy state in order to be able to channel effectively and clearly. Channelling actually has an effect and impact on the physical body. It requires a great deal of physical stamina and endurance. Hence my instinctual drive to create a healthy, robust physical body. It was not a conscious decision yet the inner drive to do this was almost compulsive.

Three years were spent researching and eating a totally raw food lifestyle. This may sound extreme yet ultimately was beneficial in many ways. Reliance on a food lifestyle consisting of vegetables, greens, fruits, nuts and seeds provided countless challenges along with opportunities to explore and expand culinary skills. One of the true benefits was the fact that upon embarking on this dietary lifestyle I initially felt extremely energized, brain fog disappeared and feelings of supreme health became evident. In time I came to recognize that such euphoric states of optimal health were the precursor to massive purging opportunities. The purges may sound gross but when I asked a lot of questions found out they were due to my body eliminating inflammation. Over time the body's defence mechanisms develop protection against the many toxic chemicals inhaled and ingested, resulting in a build-up of inflammation. The inflammation in turn creates acidity in the body, which is also the precursor to many modern day illness conditions. The purging or detox process actually supports the physical body into a healthier state. Most of the foods in the raw food lifestyle are either pH neutral or alkaline thereby supporting good health.

At age twenty-one I'd become aware that I was unfit and if care wasn't taken then my health would also deteriorate. At the same time I also had a sense that it was possible to maintain optimal health, a strong and fit body, right up until the time came to transition. An image of a nimble mountain goat had popped into mind and I realized that getting older in years didn't necessarily mean deteriorating health. I saw myself being spry, fit and agile right into very old age. This awareness was a wake-up call which resulted in immediate changes in food lifestyle along with adopting a regular fitness routine. In time the fitness routine became excessive though it was also a way of relieving inner stress. My interest in eating a healthy diet blossomed rapidly. Along the way many poor choices were made, yet each and every poor choice provided an opportunity for learning more about health, wellness and my body's unique biochemistry. Observing and feeling my body's reactions to certain foods certainly was the best indicator of whether specific foods enhanced or detracted from overall feelings of wellness.

The raw food lifestyle was possible due to the large variety of foods readily available in the States, combined with the fact that there was a large volume of information readily available on its benefits. It was at this time that a statement made by Jane during my astrology reading some years earlier resurfaced in my mind. "You would have made a great naturopath," she had said a number of times. It was during this time that my long held interest in the health and healing impact of foods became more entrenched.

It was interesting to observe that once again I was that square peg, the one that was oddly different. The majority of my colleagues, friends and clients were not interested in making dietary changes, believing that eating a diet of fast foods or food that had no life force wouldn't make any difference. Some were quite happy to embrace spiritual teachings and practices without ensuring that their physical body or emotional space was in harmony with their increasing consciousness or awareness.

This time, however, I did not feel slighted or even in the least bit different. I had reached a space of inner acceptance and valued my uniqueness, idiosyncrasies and quirkiness. My inner voice was my compass, it provided all the direction and positive or negative reinforcement needed. While it was easy to hear what others were sharing I realized that they too had their particular story, in which it was not necessary for agreement or alignment to occur in order for self-acceptance and self-worth to exist. My journey of healing the emotional wounds had truly come a long way.

"Follow your bliss and the universe will open doors where there were only walls."

Joseph Campbell

CHAPTER 16

The one thing missing in my life in the Pacific North West was connection with a specific spirit guide or community of guides. There had been no farewells exchanged with the Arcturians Their lengthy presence in my life had provided a pivotal and important learning process and I'd become used to their teaching style, which basically was one of non-communication and involved countless, non-stop experiential opportunities.

A typical mind conversation with them would be brief and non-fruitful; that is how it appeared from my perspective. In the early days of our connection I constantly asked questions about healing, energy and everything else seemingly relevant. A question would be asked and the response, loud and clear, would invariably be "All is well." Or similar responses would be "Trust", "Observe closely" or if they were especially loquacious I'd hear "In time you will understand". Being somewhat of a slow learner at times I persisted with the incessant questioning until finally realizing that mind conversation wasn't the way to learn. Instead, their powerful teaching was experiential in structure, involving a gradual process of learning that accumulated due to the different situations and opportunities that were cleverly presented.

In the education system I'd learned this method of learning was called the spiral curriculum of learning. Basically a concept is taught and experienced. This initial concept is then steadily expanded upon so that a greater complexity is eventually taught and experienced. The resultant outcome is that a solid base is created for learning and problem solving, and the student then develops a broader skill set to work with. Upon reflection the Arcturian instruction had been skilful and had served me well as my grasp of energy concepts had undergone a massive transformation in a relatively short period of time.

Despite no longer feeling the presence of the Arcturians there was still plenty of spirit guidance provided upon taking up residence in the States. This was especially evident when working with clients, when teaching and at other unexpected times. Yet, there wasn't any one particular presence sensed that would provide on-going guidance. Instead, often it felt as though I was winging it and that required a lot of acceptance and trust on my part.

One morning, upon awakening, a lightning bolt of insight poured into consciousness. "I have enough knowledge and information to write a book about healing," was the immediate and clear thought that was rammed into my head. "Mmmmm… now that's a thought." came next.

The following half an hour or so was spent trailing this thread, allowing it to begin unravelling. The more it was explored the more exciting it became as I reflected upon the vast amount of study and learning undertaken when working with the Arcturians. Their teaching, my out of this world energy experiences and all that I'd learned from working with a large, diverse client base provided a vast scope of information that might possibly be useful or relevant to other people.

Thus began twelve months of intense writing. Cloistered away in my study at every possible opportunity, generally for hours at a time, the book began to take shape. Translating what is innately known and understood into a written work that can be utilized by others for their own healing journey required considerable crafting and ingenuity. The aim of the book was to provide a straightforward 'how to' guide to self-healing on every level. What had started off as a straightforward concept gradually evolved into something that was far more complex and comprehensive. The underlying theme to every concept presented and explored was energy and the human energy body, with the ultimate aim of presenting a model for the possibility of creating a healthy energy body in order to maintain optimal health.

During this time regular work commitments also continued, while every spare moment was devoted to writing, editing and improving the manuscript. Time for sleep and social engagements were limited. This book contained my words, it was not channelled and it required intellect, careful scrutiny and ongoing editing. Initially many chapters were written, with no idea of sequence or book structure. Each chapter was largely self-contained, exploring a particular concept in great detail. The challenge then arose as to putting it together into a unified format. Chapters, like jigsaw pieces, needed to fit cohesively into a complete constructive unit. Many attempts, countless headaches and intense frustrations finally resulted in a package that felt right. The greatest achievement was that I felt as though this was my work, my accomplishment even though I had to acknowledge that some encouragement and nudges had occurred occasionally from my non-physical friends.

The whole process, from commencing writing to publication took two years of intense work. It was a labour of love and it was with both sadness and joy that its period of gestation finally manifested into its birthing. Working with an editor and publishing company provided another learning curve. The book release required a great deal of marketing and promotion.

Unfortunately it also required a visible presence from its author and that was something I was loath to undertake. The situation was explained clearly, so clearly that I would have had to have been deaf, dumb and blind to misunderstand. I loved the solitude of writing, of allowing my mind to work, to figure out and puzzle the challenges that writing presented. Writing was an intensely private and personal experience. Sharing my writing with the world meant exposing myself to the world in an unfamiliar way, and that felt both uncomfortable and threatening.

Having felt different for most of my life I'd reached the point where I was finally feeling more accepting of being in my own skin, but still uncomfortable in situations where being different might be highly noticeable. The Myers-Briggs Type Indicator that had been completed and analysed all those years earlier also indicated that my personality type was in the middle, between being an extravert and introvert with a slight leaning towards extraversion. In other words, I really wasn't significantly one or the other and that analysis possibly still held some truth. When working in the education sector my comfort level was high when teaching; it was low when addressing a larger gathering of parents or colleagues. The years spent developing my skills in the field of natural therapies had led to increased self-confidence. Yet I realized that working in a specialized field involved interacting with individuals and groups with similar interests, therefore generating a feeling of safety and ease within.

Socially I preferred small, intimate gatherings to large parties. I was not, and never had been, a party animal nor did I enjoy being the centre of attention. In fact, every opportunity to avoid being noticed had been my *modus operandi* from an early age. In the work environment my job satisfaction had always been to undertake and complete projects, working easily in the background while supporting others who were in the limelight. Maybe this resistance to being seen in the public spotlight could be attributed to a commonly shared fear of public speaking.

If only it were possible to write and be published without all the accompanying marketing that was needed. My publishing company had stressed the importance of a face being attached to the book. While I understood that particular psychology I wasn't necessarily keen to undertake the rounds of public exposure, of speaking publicly, sharing and inviting the public to become enamoured with my words of wisdom. It would require stepping far out of my comfort zone, in a way never undertaken previously. I wasn't sure of my ability to do this. Talk is one thing, and I was good at that. Action required more confidence and possibly I was all bluster. Talking a good line is different to actually following through with matching action.

Arranging a marketing schedule was easy. Co-ordinating with book stores, radio stations and sending copies to possible interested magazines for review proved effortless. My skills at working behind the scenes were well honed. Almost as much time was spent on arranging the final editing of the book, discussions with editor and working on marketing arrangements as were spent on writing the actual book. By this time I'd had the awareness that writing a book takes up fifty percent of time and energy. The remaining fifty percent is spent on getting the book published and marketed.

During this time of frenzied activity there seemed to be little, if any, communication with spirit guides. There wasn't even time to lament the lack of contact or support. By then it had become evident that at times of intense involvement in the physical reality the non-physical guides would step back and become uninvolved. Should their guidance be needed then their presence would, once again, be felt. At this point, however, attention was entirely focused on creating a full marketing plan and bringing it to fruition. Allan and I had discussed the book tour and he had decided to remain behind. This suited my plans as the arranged schedule of travel and appearances in book stores in four states and Canada was tight.

Shortly before departure date Allan informed me that he and his dog would be accompanying me on the book tour. This was not what I wanted to hear. Undertaking travel and marketing commitments on my own would be far easier. My concern was that all my attention would be needed on fulfilling my commitments and a tight schedule wouldn't allow for any distractions. Allan's reasoning for joining me sounded logical and practical. Intuitively it didn't sit comfortably; a foreboding of disaster loomed from deep within. There was nothing to be done except take the book tour one day at a time and ensure that the schedule was adhered to no matter whatever else might occur.

The first book event went extremely well and was hugely successful. Speaking to a large audience was surprisingly easy. All those fears of being seen centre stage were erroneous. I felt extremely comfortable and loved every minute spent in front of an audience. Even the challenging or difficult questions hadn't been a deterrent. On that first night of sharing my experiences publicly I recognized an aspect of myself that had been well hidden. This aspect wasn't ego, or so I hoped. Instead I had publicly acknowledged and shared my knowledge in a way that hopefully was meaningful and enriching to the audience. At the end of the evening feelings of euphoria and excitement were predominant. Speaking publicly wasn't difficult. It seemed effortless and most importantly I felt completely at ease in this new role.

Unfortunately the euphoria lasted only a few short hours. The following day necessitated a long drive, which was where things between Allan and I really began to go wrong. And the tone was then set for the remaining time on the road, with one difficulty after the next interfering with the intention of the tour. We'd set out early and it wasn't long before the first incident occurred. Roadworks on the highway resulted in reduced speed limit signs being well posted in advance and along the way. Several times I indicated the change in speed limit to Allan, which he duly ignored. Shortly after my ignored attempts a police officer pulled him over for exceeding the posted speed limit. Allan was not contrite and the ensuing discussion between them was markedly hostile. Allan simmered afterwards and finally turned toward me and angrily said, "What happened to your spirit guides? They should have warned that this might happen!"

"Mmmmm, three times I indicated clearly that the speed limit had changed. Isn't that sufficient warning?"

My response was followed by an unrepeatable tirade, with his final comment on the subject being, "You drive then." Compliance followed, my reasoning being that it was easier to do so rather than aggravate his bad mood. Sometimes it's easier to be amenable in order to have peace, all the while I hoped and almost prayed fervently that this would be the only mishap on the trip. Regardless it seemed as if the universe was conspiring against me because shortly afterwards there was another mishap and by this time the energy between us roller coasted between being Arctic and fiery as hell. Allan's anger escalated and he insisted that I stop the vehicle so he could get out and he would find his own way home. At this particular point we were many hours from home and it was not my intention to drive his large vehicle for the remainder of the trip. Instead, I indicated that I'd be happy for him to go home once we reached the next destination on my schedule. He could take himself, the dog and his truck and I'd hire a rental vehicle for the remainder of my book tour.

It was late when we reached the motel that I'd booked in advance. There was snow on the ground and the town in the hills seemed sleepy and shut down for the day as I nosed the truck into a parking bay outside the motel. "We'll sort out the arrangements first thing in the morning. Once I get a hire vehicle then you head back and I'll continue on," was my comment prior to collapsing into bed, too exhausted by the stressful day to say more. The following morning Allan seemed calmer and almost immediately upon waking up he informed me that he would accompany me for the remainder of my book tour. "Oh oh," I thought, "this can only mean more dramas and stresses."

Early in the marriage I'd learned that Allan possessed a mercurial temperament, a complete contrast to my more even-tempered attitude towards life. They say that opposites attract and I will admit that often I questioned the mind-set of the person who had initially made that so-called observation or discovery! Overall, my reservations about having Allan accompany me on this long trip were well proven. A litany of comments and complaints accompanied the whole trip. "We need to upgrade to higher quality motels." "I need to spend time resting and recovering from the non-stop travel." "What's the hurry?" "There's nothing like enjoying a vacation and having someone else pay for it."

And so on it went. I lost count of the number of times I reiterated that I'd shared, prior to heading out, that this trip had an incredibly tight schedule and that it was being undertaken on a shoe-string budget. Both those bits of vitally important information seemed to have totally escaped his memory, despite my constant reminders along the trip.

Physically, mentally and emotionally spent we eventually arrived home. My schedule had been adhered to, with some difficulty, constant dramas and conflicts. Regardless I was pleased with the overall results; the book tour had gone well and my confidence in doing presentations had increased greatly. Interestingly the greatest satisfaction had been meeting and interacting with people of different backgrounds and interests. Any book sales made were of lesser importance. I revelled in my new-found ability to mix with people comfortably, and I especially was relieved to find that public speaking was actually enjoyable.

There was one highlight of the journey that to this day still fills me with awe and wonder. Early one morning I slipped out of the motel room, with Allan's dog by my side, and we went for a walk along a beachside esplanade. The sun was shining, the blue sky couldn't have been clearer. People were everywhere, exercising and enjoying the early morning sunshine. We'd gone for a long walk, which made a welcome change from the endless hours spent driving and sitting. As we neared the motel I began to feel emotions of resistance about continuing this journey called marriage with Allan.

Suddenly there was a loud, unfamiliar sound all around. I stopped walking, wondering what in the world was happening. Next thing, a massive flock of pigeons flapped noisily around both the dog and myself. She stood completely still, which was totally out of character for the usually energetic dog. I was immobile also. The beating of the wings and the loud noise made by the flapping motion eventually abated and the whole flock of pigeons gracefully and gently settled down upon the grass, fully encircling us. We were mesmerized. People passing by stared, disbelieving what had unexpectedly occurred. The energy was surreal and instinctively I knew this was a gift from spirit.

Nevertheless, upon returning home my mind was made up. My marriage was over. The frequent anger outbursts, the stress involved in maintaining my balance was too difficult. Allan's constant need for reassurance was draining. It wasn't possible to officially end the marriage and so it continued on, a marriage in name only. Separate sleeping arrangements worked well and gradually I focused once more on finding meaning in my work, immersing myself in new challenges and opportunities for further growth.

It was around this time that the presence of spirit guides once again became more evident. I began to notice their soft energy signature around me more frequently and also saw them out of the corner of my eyes. In fact, I'd often see them moving about as though they lived in the same house! My mind in turmoil I questioned the reasons for my marriage and the possibility of ending it officially. Earlier in the marriage I'd been told by non-physical beings that the marriage would not be long lasting. This information had been provided after the wedding band had been placed on my ring finger.

For over ten years I'd been fortunate to receive this type of guidance in advance of specific events occurring. I'd been alerted of numerous changes that would occur, always without any indication of time or even reason. Armed with the knowledge that the marriage had a short shelf life I regularly asked, "Is it time to tell him?" This question was asked mentally after every argument, intense disagreement or after hearing further verbal outbursts of frustration or anger. For six months after the book tour I heard the same reply repeated too often. "No." Hearing that one word response was sufficient reason to take no action, and so I kept quiet about my inner disquiet and knowing, despite the fact that I'd come to feel as though I was walking on eggshells in the relationship.

There were always reasons for timing and happenings and once again it was a matter of living in trust and with patience. I knew that change would happen when it was meant to just as I finally knew that I would be fully guided onto whatever was meant to happen next.

"You stop explaining yourself when you realize people only understand from their level of perception."

Jim Carrey

CHAPTER 17

Like most people I'd grown up believing that marriage involved a commitment, which was to love and honour, in sickness and in health, for better or worse and so on. Marriage was meant to be for life. Walking away from my first marriage had not been undertaken lightly. In fact, it had been an excruciatingly difficult decision to make; a decision that had been made out of a desperate need for survival. I'd become aware, once I'd adjusted to and accepted my new life in the healing arts field, that if I'd remained in the first marriage I would have died an early death from breast cancer. This awareness arose about five years after leaving the marriage. By then I'd become fully aware of the impact of unresolved emotional issues on physical health. The whole Body, Mind, Spirit connection had been a revelation as previously I'd believed that eating healthy and exercising were all that was needed to ward off illness conditions.

Observing my second marriage disintegrate was catastrophic. I questioned my ability to choose wisely, fought with inner demons about my ability to love and be loved and all the other countless irrational thoughts that accompany any committed relationship breakdown. When my first marriage ended someone had reassuringly said, "Divorce is not about failure, it's about change". At the time I took those words seriously and held onto them as an indication of positive change and growth. Now, with my second marriage rapidly approaching disintegration even those words weren't sufficient reason to feel calm acceptance.

Like practically everyone else in society I'd always believed in true love and that everyone had the right, and even need, to be in a loving committed relationship. In particular, such a relationship was dignified and signified through the rites of marriage. I'd subscribed to the notion that relationships and marriage were not only important for personal growth but were an essential component of having the human experience. All that had been read and discussed on the subject affirmed this belief. Countless times after a relationship ended I'd been told by numerous colleagues and friends that there was a man coming into my life, as if that was the solution to whatever possible need might exist within me. I had never questioned this perception of reality; had assumed that this is what each soul incarnated for, that each relationship provided an opportunity for further learning and growth. So, like everyone else going through relationship breakdown I had feelings of failure and inadequacy; convinced that possibly maybe in some distant future I'd get this relationship thing right. Not once did I question the validity of the shared cultural beliefs and practices around the necessity and importance of marriage.

Years later I read *Committed: A Love Story* by Elizabeth Gilbert which was more of a sociological perspective on marriage in different cultures rather than being a romance novel. Her questioning and research came to the ultimate and well documented conclusion that marriage in our society was a control mechanism (my words) used by the state or government to keep a check on its population. Marriage may be sanctified by a religious order but in reality it's a state control mechanism. This conclusion resonated deeply and gradually another truth dawned, one that I'd never anticipated.

Sometimes a truth or revelation can spring upon awareness without any warning, and in doing so can be confronting or alarming. Or, it may dawn slowly with little hint of its ultimate importance. The latter was the case in my situation. After my second marriage ended I swore I'd never marry again and in fact shunned any potential for a relationship for many years. This wasn't because of fear, hatred or dislike of the opposite sex. It was merely the way things unfolded, as other things demanded focus, time and attention. The simple revelation when it arrived was surprising. It was basically that, at a deeper or soul level, I had incarnated into this body to lead a spiritual life; that I had other tasks to perform and in order to complete them my attention needed to be fully involved there.

Upon delving deeper within it became apparent that subconsciously I'd absorbed the programming, or beliefs of society around the necessity of finding true love, and that being in a committed relationship was essential not only to wellbeing but also it ensured acceptance within the larger community. Being one half of a couple meant fitting in with acceptable norms and behaviours. The implication of doing otherwise meant that there was something inherently wrong if I wasn't fulfilling my obligation in this regard. Literature, media advertising and myths handed down through the generations espoused the importance, validity and necessity of this belief. I'd lived my life unconsciously accepting this belief, which was no more than a lie. Marriage is not for everyone; it is not the be all of existence as I was rapidly coming to understand.

∞∞∞∞

The reason for being guided to remain married for a while longer became apparent a few months later. It came unexpectedly and resulted in more questions than answers, which is always the case when working with spirit energy and wisdom.

With countless acupuncture needles sticking out of every conceivable place on my face, in addition to several other parts of my body, my appearance surely resembled that of a porcupine. A few weeks earlier I had signed up to have a series of ten facial rejuvenation sessions with my favourite acupuncturist, Gabi, and had gradually become accustomed to the sensation of needles piercing my skin. By this stage I had learned to relax and enjoy this totally different and peaceful experience. Having the needles inserted no longer provoked any feelings of anxiety, merely anticipation, as a session was as relaxing as a lengthy meditation.

On this particular day while totally relaxing and feeling as though I did not have a care in the world I became aware of a cool sensation over my third eye, which according to Eastern spiritual teachings is located in the middle of the forehead. This slight sensation felt like a gentle hand or breeze moving over the area. Upon mentioning this to Gabi she commented that it was Edgar Cayce. By this stage my body felt totally dissociated from my consciousness and all I was capable of doing was feeling and loosely observing what was happening. I couldn't actually rouse myself sufficiently to move, though there was sufficient awareness that moving my body with all those acupuncture needles stuck in it might not be such a good idea. Instead I remained as calm as possible and continued scanning the sensations.

As well as being a highly skilled acupuncturist Gabi was also a shaman and a gifted intuitive. She commented that the energy of Edgar Cayce working on my third eye was expanding my third eye vortex in addition to making some energy connections with something deep in my brain, accessing an area that is not normally accessed in humans. None of this information made much, if any, sense given my meditative Zen state. In truth, it didn't make much sense later on when I was able to reflect on its occurrence.

Forcing myself to shift slightly from my deep state of relaxation I asked her about Edgar Cayce. Why was his energy present? What did it signify? How did she even know it was Edgar Cayce? And, there were many questions that could have been asked but somehow my brain functioning seemed to be impaired due to the delightfully tranquil state the acupuncture treatment was inducing. As an acupuncturist Gabi had a sound knowledge of Traditional Chinese Medicine and other related healing modalities. As an intuitive she readily acknowledged her ability to receive information from the other side. On many previous occasions Edgar Cayce had provided information to assist her in working with clients.

As I lay there motionless, having dozed off into that Zen state once again, I felt the energy working around my head for a while. Then suddenly a surge of strong energy moved directly into my solar plexus.

"Gabi, something's moving into my solar plexus," I mumbled as I endeavoured to focus. The sensation was neither uncomfortable nor comfortable – it felt like a rush of energy moving downwards into my body. In my line of work I had become very familiar with spirit energies, as well as understanding and being sensitive to energy, and was accustomed to energy surges occurring from time to time.

"It's Edgar Cayce," she responded.

"What's he doing? I can feel his energy coming into my body. It's spreading outwards. Why is this happening?"

Before Gabi could respond I suddenly felt this energy flow moving all through my body and begin to merge with mine. My legs lifted off the table effortlessly, and uncontrollably, and my whole body moved in paroxysms as the energy slotted within mine. Gabi commented that she could see my body adjust and change to accommodate this energy. Surprisingly the acupuncture needles remained in place even with all the uncontrollable erratic movement.

His adjusting to my body was not without discomfort. It resulted in quite a lot of shifting and stretching of my body to accommodate what distinctly felt like a lengthier frame. However, his energy remained and every now and then over the next couple of weeks I found myself stretching unconsciously, as though my body were being stretched for me. Intuitively I sensed that his energy was adjusting to the constraints of a smaller energy body.

During this time my awareness of his energy strengthened. My sense of him was that he was of slight and slim build and was taller than me. He wore regular trousers (often grey) and usually a light coloured shirt. His hair was sandy, light brown. It must be admitted that at this stage my knowledge of the life of Edgar Cayce was very limited. Years earlier I had read a couple of books about his life. Since that time I had not encountered any of the literature around his trance readings nor did I hold any perception, one way or the other, of this man who had been hailed as the Father of Holistic Medicine.

Initially the energy of Edgar Cayce felt overwhelmingly predominant within me. My early understanding was that this was to be a melding of two energies, which was occurring for a higher purpose. Needless to say, this experience was not without challenges and discomfort along the way. On a conscious level there was a realization that life would never be the same. It brought to mind a whole slew of questions and concerns. How would my life become different? What would this merging of two energies produce? Would I lose my sense of self? And, ultimately would I become totally submerged into this new energy? Thoughts around loss of self-control and self-identity whizzed around my head for months. Yet, on another level there was a feeling of excitement, a sense of a new adventure about to commence.

I sensed that this next chapter of my life would involve channelling the energy of Edgar Cayce. Normally when channelling spirit energy there is a point where the entity would enter my energy field and would remain there only for the duration of the channelling. This as yet undefined experience with the energy of Edgar Cayce was unique and unusual as his energy seemed to be permanently lodged within me. It was disconcerting and brought up a lot of uncertainty and even some unexpected fears. As always, though, I managed to put on a brave face, acting as if this was normal and wasn't in the least bit intimidating.

In my journaling I wrote: "I welcome you Edgar. I feel joyous when I think of you. I know this path is not without its attendant risks, yet I know that I truly am safe and protected." Maybe this was meant as a way of reassuring myself, or it could possibly have been sheer bravado, something I'd become extremely adept at doing over the years. However, from this simple beginning a long and intense period of study (on my part) and teaching (from him) commenced.

I heard his voice clearly, his response was very direct: *"Right now you are overawed, are you not? There is no need to be, for this is perfect, a union of two souls who are focused on bringing forth new information of high levels. The timing is perfect. It will not be long before you begin the process of actually merging our energies into the one. Almost there but not quite and it is only a matter of some congruence occurring, in terms of timing. You may think it is a simple matter to conjoin two powerful energies. It is not, as there is retrieval and interaction of material - much like data processing. All the information has to be brought forward in order for it to be fully synthesized. When this happens, then, and only then, will the full force of the combined knowledge and skills be felt. This will revolutionize the way many people think and believe. Aaaahhhhh you are tired. It takes some adjusting, does it not? It will help if you cooperate and allow your body some rest time! Go now and relax and you will find yourself feeling renewed and more vital."*

How correct he was. Tiredness was one of the constant symptoms that became immediately apparent during the merging process, and which continued on and off at different times during our joint journey. Often it was more than mere tiredness; it became mind numbing exhaustion for intervals of time.

Two weeks after that initial melding there was further adjustment during my next treatment with Gabi. This time the energy of Edgar Cayce was in charge. He gave directions, via Gabi, as to what needed to be cleared, straightened or released energetically from my body. A number of significant modifications were made to my energy body. These changes were instituted to enhance my intuitive ability, which was always used extensively in my healing practice. Whether these energy changes would in any way impact my physical body and its functioning was not initially obvious. In time, however, it became apparent that my physical body would be heavily affected by the energy changes.

Over a period of eighteen months considerable fine-tuning of the subtle energies in my body occurred. At times the energy of Edgar

Cayce was highly prevalent in my life, and at other times it seemed as though his energy was not discernible. However, that eighteen-month period of gestating the energy of Edgar was a time of profound inner change and growth, with Edgar continually teaching and guiding me. Additionally, there were energetic changes within my body that at times had physical ramifications.

∞∞∞∞

Within a few months of first encountering and melding with the energy of Edgar Cayce my marriage entered its final throes. The ending of any relationship is never enjoyable and can often be unpleasant. Allan and I certainly exchanged words on occasion but overall it seemed as though we both felt regret that the relationship had come to this. Our parting was filled with good wishes for the other. We hugged farewell and I made my way to the North East and he headed south and on to a new life. The formalities of property settlement and divorce had been dealt with amicably and efficiently. It was with both excitement and hesitation that I began the long drive across country. There was no idea of what awaited me. Once again I was cast adrift into new and unknown territory. This time, however, my inner grit and determination were stronger and well honed, more so than previously.

"You are here to enable the divine purpose of the universe to unfold. That is how important you are."

Eckhart Tolle

CHAPTER 18

A new chapter dawned. I was filled with excitement at the prospect of potential opportunities for exploring the North East. Many Australians love the idea of spending time in the States, and I actually had the good fortune to be living there. How long would this opportunity last? I had absolutely no idea but one thing was certain; there was still more to come. Upstate New York is stunning; in fact the whole state has many incredible vistas to see and explore.

Luckily I'd learned a great deal from previous experiences in the Pacific North West so that establishing a business on the East Coast wasn't as difficult as anticipated. By this stage I'd learned that intention and enthusiasm were necessary for goal achievement and when combined with unstoppable determination then anything was possible. Also, by then I'd become fully aware that if something was meant to be, then it would happen. If it wasn't meant to be then any effort applied would be wasted energy and would be met with resistance.

The initial encounter with the energy of Edgar Cayce had occurred only a few months previously so I wasn't too sure what to expect upon arrival on the East coast. How would this melded energy impact my life? Were those earlier experiences only the beginning of something more or would they fizzle out to nothing? My initial priority was to settle into a new life and to establish myself in business. The bottom line was that income needed to be earned and sooner rather than later!

Practitioners of energy medicine (or vibrational medicine as it's often called) understand fully that when changes occur energetically they may, in time, manifest in the physical body. One such instance took place in my body a few months after moving to the East coast. I experienced what appeared to be discomforting vertigo episodes, lasting about five to seven days altogether. My immediate thinking was that my blood pressure had dropped significantly, and that thought was strongly reinforced as it was difficult to find a strong pulse at times.

Whenever I attempt to problem solve issues or concerns it is a normal practice to begin asking a lot of questions of my spirit guides who have, over the years, provided valuable insight and guidance in countless areas. Since the integration with Edgar Cayce's energy I had come to rely on his responses to requests for information. In this particular situation, with vertigo episodes occurring innumerable times each day, all my questioning resulted in the same response. My physical health was not the cause, nor was my health at risk. And I definitely did not have a brain tumour, despite asking if that was the case multiple times.

A few days after the onset of the distressing and uncomfortable vertigo symptoms I heard three distinct words, "blood thinning out". These words popped into my head as I was taking my daily early morning walk. This walk, though, was not undertaken in a brisk and determined manner. Due to the distinct sensations of imbalance in my body it was actually more of a stagger or stumble. From those three words an immediate knowing and understanding flowed through into my consciousness

My blood was being thinned. I ascertained that this thinning of the blood was a physical necessity, and was in response to the ongoing energy changes that had been taking place in my body's energy field for countless years. The melding with Edgar Cayce's energy no doubt also contributed to changes within. In order to hold a higher vibration there ultimately has to be some manifestation of this change on the physical level. Regular and ongoing healing work on the energy levels must at some stage result in changes to the denser physical body. In theory, this made sense. Nevertheless it was disconcerting to actually have a physical change occur so dramatically and unexpectedly. Ironically years later different clients reported similar vertigo episodes occurring.

At the time I was curious as to why thinning of the blood occurred. Again, almost immediately a slew of information flowed into consciousness. Blood is transported to all parts of the body. Its viscosity has to match the overall energy vibration, or frequency, held by the body. The Central Nervous System is also connected to the cardiovascular system. Information travels through the body via the cellular structure (blood cells, nerve cells, etc). DNA information is stored and communicated via the cardiovascular system. And, most importantly, oxygen is transported via the blood cells. Ayurvedic medicine teaches that *prana* (breath) holds life. In other words, energy (breath or life force) is circulated freely throughout the body via the respiration process, which of course is connected to the cardiovascular system.

As the body ages and is weighed down with illness, worry and other human conditions there is a thickening in blood viscosity. It becomes sluggish and prone to clotting and embolisms. With natural blood thinning, due to increasing vibrational frequency, there is a reversal of many of the aging tendencies. This results in increased energy levels, improvement in processing of bodily functions as well as improved inter- and intra-cellular functioning.

This was only one of the changes experienced during an eighteen-month period. Another change that was incredibly challenging was to empty the mind of thought. Edgar Cayce constantly reminded me of the importance of this practice. Every time I thought this near impossible skill was mastered he gently reminded me that there was still some way to go. It was intensely difficult to suddenly shift into a state of non-thought at all times. In fact, it was downright impossible due to the fact that western culture venerates logic and reasoning, something that I'd been rather adept at employing for a large part of my life.

The ability to silence the mind is given little or no importance in most day to day interactions or conversations. However, Edgar stressed the necessity of training myself to be in this state, as it would enable us to work together more effortlessly. Was I able to master the art of living in a non-thought state at all times? Definitely not, though it became more effortless over time and after three years of intense practice there was significant improvement.

A telepathic communication from Edgar provided an indication of the journey that had been embarked upon. He commented:

"Good progress is being made. There is yet more for you to experience before you will feel fully comfortable working with these energies I hold. You see, there has to be a perfect balance. Though we are all One we each hold different frequencies. In order for the harmonization of our frequencies to work to a high standard there has to be this balancing act. Visualize a see-saw. Up and down it goes until at some point it stabilizes in the middle. It is that point we are working towards. Your mind is emptying. Still more

to go, much more to go. Continue, continue with this work. It is vitally important that you come to a state of non-thought.

It is indeed a magnificent blending of the two energies. I ask for your cooperation. I will not coerce you. I will speak to you. I do this not out of a selfish desire to control you, nor would I in any way wish to interfere with or impede your karma. No, no, no, you know only too well as do I that this arrangement between us – I will not refer to it as a contract – no, no, it is an agreement between two willing souls that this arrangement is for the higher good of all. My purpose at all times is to be of service.

So this joining together of two energies that have the same aspiration to be of service produces an energy that is far greater than the individuals themselves could possibly produce. You are the vehicle upon which I will bring the information that could not be shared at the time I incarnated. You are the vehicle that has agreed to be entrusted with this task."

As was the normal practice when connecting and working with a new spirit guide or community of guides, there was a period of time where it felt as though very little, if anything was actually happening. I was busy establishing myself as a professional in the area, meeting other practitioners and creating professional credibility with clients. Edgar didn't disappear. In fact, his presence was felt most often at night. Just as I was about to fall asleep his energy would become evident and then his voice would be heard. It mainly felt as though he was whispering in my ear. Often the wealth of information he provided was prodigious. He was my personal life coach, teacher and mentor rolled into the one consciousness. His presence was also sensed when I was working with clients, as his knowledge would guide my work when and where he obviously felt it necessary.

If there's one thing I've learned it's to fully accept and trust the voices that were heard in my head. I've never been urged to do harm to myself or others. The words of wisdom have always been spoken with simplicity and over time I've found them to be reliable, insightful and truthful. Interestingly each spirit guide or community that I've had the honour to work with possessed a unique and distinctive voice, language structure and semantic usage. Often archaic words were heard; sometimes syntax was different or unusual. In fact, I've not heard language expressed in the way that I speak or think. In every instance it's been distinctly different and often interestingly expressed.

While I was aware there was a likelihood that at some stage I would be channelling the words of Edgar there wasn't any indication or hurry around this happening. This is an aspect of spirit connection that I greatly appreciate. Edgar was assisting in preparing my physical body for what was ahead. A relationship ending combined with moving house to the other side of the country had placed a great deal of stress upon my body, despite my repeated assertions to the contrary. The whole process had been far more stressful than anticipated and my body needed time to heal and regain its equilibrium. Additionally, there was still further adjustment and acceptance of this weird commingling of souls. His energy held a high frequency. Mine, being somewhat mired in human consciousness wasn't at such an elevated level. That in itself required a great deal of adjustment, especially on my part.

My initial disquiet around the merging of the two energies quickly dissipated even though the process involved ongoing discomfort, even pain, in the early stages. His higher energy acted as a catalyst for changes to occur in my body. The old and heavy energy within needed to be released as it didn't resonate with, or wasn't on the same wavelength, as the new energy infusion. Any pain experienced was largely due to the old energy memories leaving my body.

As Edgar succinctly expressed, *"Your eagerness is evident and you are well prepared. However, there are some aspects of your physiology that really are not quite in readiness. For example, your central nervous system is over stimulated. Not so much by things that are occurring in your life at this present moment, but more so from the memories stored within and from DNA that is affecting the whole central nervous system."*

There is no doubt that the higher energy infusion from the merging of energies resulted in further stress on my body's functioning. This resulted in heightened sensitivity in many areas of functioning such as smell, hearing, feeling etc. During this time I questioned intently the whereabouts of the Edgar Cayce energy located within my body. I felt this presence constantly and definitely more keenly when working with clients or teaching. When those tasks were finished the feeling of his expanded energy within seemed to gently withdraw. It took time but eventually I became aware of how the energy merging actually functioned.

His energy sat or was present as a thirty centimetre (twelve inches) filament of light energy in the mid-spine area of my back. This is the area commonly referred to as the Kundalini in ancient spiritual teachings. When working with clients or teaching I felt that energy expand from within to encompass about two-thirds of my body. As an energy sensation it was gentle yet very distinct. Later on, when channelling his words I felt this energy expand well beyond both my physical body and energy field.

Another explanation from Edgar about the energy shifts occurring related to the strengthening of my voice box. This strengthening of the voice box occurred on the subtle levels and was in preparation for the channelling work still ahead.

"It is important in your physical body to have balance, to be steadfast and to have strength. The work you and I are about to undertake will involve long hours, intense concentration and a great deal of personal interaction. Your voice box, which is currently being prepared for this work is not yet ready. You will no doubt have noticed yourself clearing your throat constantly. You may think this is the beginning of a cold but this is not the case. No, no, this is indeed your voice box that is strengthening. As you are aware your vocal cords require a lot of liquids in order to function really well and to be able to function at optimal levels for long periods of time. It is important to continually keep your physiology well hydrated. If you do not then you will find over-exertion takes place. Should that occur you are likely to suffer inflammation and weakening. This is not a desired outcome. While you are asleep and other moments when you are not exercising your vocal cords you will find you will go 'hrmmmp' from time to time because there are threads, golden threads that are being interwoven all through your vocal cords. This is to support you in the work that is about to commence."

This commentary is a clear explanation of the complexity that exists within the energy body. The energy body is fluid, it changes and modifies according to the frequency held by an individual. It was one of a number of similar explanations provided by Edgar during our time together.

There was no doubt about it; I definitely did not need another relationship partner or husband. Edgar was on my case sufficiently for me, at times, to consider his tutelage to be another form of nagging. His persistent reminders about being fully present in the moment, living in a state of non-thought had become somewhat of a mental mantra, though naturally my achievement fell short of aspirations for a long while. Regular meditation routine was completely discarded. Going cold turkey wasn't easy as I'd grown to relish and value those quality times of relaxation and restoration. Nevertheless a new practice of conscious and focused breathing was instituted. This involved timing myself, initially for very short periods such as two or three minutes where I would mentally say, "Inhale, Circulate, Exhale" as the breath did exactly that in my body. The reason for starting with such a basic technique was to train my body to eventually feel and carry out this process naturally. I realized that breathing had become such an automatic response that awareness of breath had completely ceased. It was time to become mindful of breath and its movement throughout my body.

Two to three minutes is a very, very long time when clock watching. Eventually this increased to five minutes, and the process was undertaken numerous times throughout the day. My impatience was strong. Something as simple as fully feeling the breath should be easy to carry out all the time. It wasn't. Eventually there was improvement and it was cause for celebration when the three words, "Inhale, Circulate, Exhale" were no longer needed.

Finally, I was ready to test my ability to focus fully on the breath and be in a space of non-thought for an extended period of time. A trip into nearby mountains, which normally would take one hour, was my target. Prior to leaving home my self-talk went along these lines, "Remember to observe without mental comments or judgments. Focus solely on what is occurring in the moment. Observe and then let it go." There's nothing quite like a solid pep talk to set the mood. Prior to this the longest period of non-thought undertaken had been fifteen minutes. My plan was ambitious but it was time to test the value of doing this, as I'd already experienced its benefits in numerous small ways.

The drive was uneventful, and though its duration was always one hour in length on this particular day it took less than fifty minutes. Eventually I came to see the tremendous value in living consciously in a state of non-thought. Overall, I'd rate focused breathing as being far more effective than meditation. In meditation it's the right brain that is dominant and induces the feelings of wellbeing and relaxation. Generally these feelings only last for as long as the stresses of life don't intrude. With focused breathing I found it also induced a relaxed state; one that could be maintained for longer, often the best part of a whole day. A huge benefit is that it could be undertaken with both eyes open and while fully functioning in everyday life. With experimentation I also discovered it to be a wonderful tool when driving. Traffic lights turned green consistently upon approach and traffic flow seemed easier to navigate. However, once thoughts intruded lights would turn red, more braking was required and other drivers were likely to suddenly change lanes and impede the ease of the journey.

Edgar, however, expressed the benefits more succinctly.

"You practice being in the moment as I have asked you. You practice the non-thought state as I have also requested. Yes. It is interesting. You are finding that as you concentrate on being in a state of non-thought, what happens? Thoughts come in and you have correctly identified those thoughts as coming from your subconscious. This is a real learning experience. You will find that you will be able to go into that state of non-thought, not only through your consciousness but also through your subconscious. It is through this awareness and practice you will eventually find there is a completely clear channel between you and Source – between you and God. It is as simple as that.

So this is the process you are now undertaking. You are being cleared of the energy, the vibration, which is causing the interference to occur when it comes to receiving direct information. It is vitally important for your channels to be totally clear on the conscious and subconscious levels. We have just made a start on this today by offering your subconscious to go into that higher state. Closing it down is not necessary. Please continue the practice of being in the state of non-thought and then when your subconscious kicks in just gently and lovingly remind it to go into a state of non-thought. In a very short period of time there will be non-thought of both conscious and subconscious."

"Every being is the author of his own health or disease."

Buddha

CHAPTER 19

An incident occurred just a few weeks after moving to New York state that was unnerving and even alarming. It presented a mystery and at the time there was no obvious outcome evident. However, nine years later a much more comprehensive understanding of that particular incident finally occurred.

For a significant part of my life I'd experienced intense stomach pains. Visits to the doctor in earlier years resulted in tests and endoscopies being performed, which had shown absolutely no abnormalities. Apparently this was one of those cases where there was no physical indication of any illness condition despite consistent pain symptoms being present. Shortly after arriving in my new abode I awoke one morning with bleeding gums and blisters throughout my mouth. There had been no previous indication of anything wrong in terms of dental hygiene. There certainly hadn't been anything amiss the night before. Being intuitive I checked in with my body as to what was occurring. The mental conversation went along these lines:

"Do I need to go to the doctor?"

"No."

"Do I need to visit a dentist?"

"No."

"Is what is happening in my mouth a physical condition?"

"No."

"Is it energetic?"

"Yes."

"Will it heal naturally?"

"Yes."

"What is happening? Why?"

There was no response to those last two questions. The silence indicated that a process of deduction would be needed. This obviously left only one possibility – in my mind anyway – that there was some energetic release process occurring even though it was manifesting as a physical condition. My relief was great as at that stage I didn't know of any doctors or dentists in the area. I had only been living there a short time and the thought of medical intervention didn't sit well. At this point in time Edgar's presence wasn't strongly evident either. My connection with Edgar at this time, though still relatively new, had been established and it was frustrating that just when I needed further insight or clarification he was definitely absent! There was no option but to remain sequestered in my apartment as I didn't relish wandering out and about in the wider world with a mouth that looked hideous and as if it were contagious. My mouth definitely was not a pretty sight to behold.

Several days later, early in the morning I was in that in-between state of not being fully awake yet no longer in deep sleep when suddenly a whole barrage of information flowed into my awareness. To this day I can still hear the information being clearly and loudly enunciated. The information stated clearly, "Your name was Lisette. You lived in Belgium during World War II and worked for the Resistance, and were the mistress of a German official. You were caught. Rather than betray the Resistance you swallowed a cyanide pill".

While the wording of the message may not have been exactly as stated, this summary is exact in terms of the message content. Immediately I knew that the bloodied mouth blisters were cellular memory being released from that cyanide poisoning. I also intuitively had the awareness that the intense stomach pains experienced on and off during my adult years were also related or connected to this information.

Another important factor relating to this episode was that since childhood I'd experienced nightmares, all around the same theme. In the nightmares I was always in the woods or forests, hiding from soldiers and leading people away from the soldiers. Never in any recurring dream was I caught. However, the feeling of extreme danger was prevalent in the nightmare. As well, over the period of my adult years I'd been obsessively fascinated by any written material or films that detailed the atrocities that occurred and were perpetrated by the Germans during World War II. Watching the movie, *Schindler's List*, was a horrific experience. It unnerved me in inexplicable ways and I felt sick to my stomach at many of the scenes. As well, any stories relating to resistance fighters caught my immediate attention, and I had also gone through a stage of watching every possible DVD that dealt with stories about the Resistance fighters. Ironically, after receiving the information relating to the reason for blistered and bloodied mouth two things happened. The nightmares ceased and my interest in learning more about resistance fighters and the Nazi treatment of them also came to an abrupt end. It felt as though I'd finally put to rest a memory that had plagued my subconscious for most of this life.

My understanding is that young children, generally up to the age of five years are most likely to have recall of other lifetimes. Usually after the age of approximately seven years children are fully immersed in their current life and any memories of previous lives have faded greatly. However, the painstaking work of psychiatrists Michael Newton, Brian Weiss and others indicates that memories can be brought to the surface during hypnosis regression sessions. There have also been countless reports of young children who are able to remember vividly details of other lives that have been lived.

Nearly ten years later I didn't anticipate the possibility of having any recall of Lisette's life in wartime Belgium. This particular story or memory remnant had been resolved, or so I thought. Regardless I was fully receptive to the idea of further exploration should there be anything else to uncover. With this possibility in mind I began reading books and viewing DVDs relating to German occupation during World War II again. In particular my focus was on events and personalities involved in the underground resistance, as well as possible key German figures.

Being gifted with psychic abilities I sensed or felt that there might just be the likelihood of flashbacks and memories surfacing. I was open to any and all possibilities, and fuelled by a determination to learn and understand as much as possible about Lisette's life, regardless of its possible brevity.

One instance where a memory was triggered occurred early on during the research period, which was undertaken during a long, wet and miserable winter. My partner at the time and I had commenced watching *Secret Army*, a BBC forty-two episode series, which depicted the Lifeline set up by an individual code named 'Yvette' in Brussels and which managed to get a large number of pilots shot down by the German military back to England. This particular Lifeline was committed to only rescuing and returning airmen, and was not in any way involved in resistance, retaliatory or sabotage activities though at times the Lifeline workers interacted with different resistance groups. The *Secret Army* series, filmed in 1977, 1978 and 1979, was riveting viewing. There were numerous instances when I felt my body tense, clench in fear or tension or react in subtle ways to the scenes. *Secret Army* was based on true life events, and some of the characters depicted in fact existed. As much as possible the series reflected actual incidents and personalities.

My partner was keen to explore further the possibility that Lisette may have been involved in the rescue and return of airmen to Britain. He used dowsing as a means of determining the validity of this possibility. Dowsing, when done correctly and with precision is a wonderful tool for determining truths and possibilities. It's a tool only, one that I've found to be reasonably reliable in providing accurate information. Anyhow, dowsing around the possibility of Lisette's involvement in the Lifeline came up negative. My partner commented questioningly, "I'm getting that Lisette wasn't involved with the Lifeline". My immediate response was blurted out, "She worked with the Communists in the Resistance. Her father was a staunch Communist so it became a family affair. Oh, and her uncle was also a Communist."

How did I know this? How reliable was this piece of information? Was there any way to verify it? Our conversation continued from there. By this stage I was in full flight, the words spilling out of my mouth of their own volition. "Communism in that time would now be viewed more as Socialism. The reason for the appeal of Communism was that its ideology was about equality, with everyone being equal, being viewed and receiving equally. The people were fed up with the authorities, with the class system and with the elite being privileged while the rest of society was often denied basic rights." Basically I went on in this vein for quite some time, very clear in my mind that the fervour of early Communism was the beginning of breaking away from the established class system. Here I must stress that I consciously had no knowledge of this, that I'd never studied Communism doctrine or manifestos.

Further research into the life of Lisette indicated that her real name was Marie-Louise Romu. She was born in July 1924 and died in Birkenau Concentration Camp in 1943. Her code name in the Resistance was

Lisette. Secrecy around identity was essential for survival. Possibly she may have been recruited by the French. She was directly involved in the sabotage of infrastructure, including the killing of Germans. Lisette was the mistress of a German Kommandant, possibly when in the concentration camp. She was betrayed by Belgium citizens, which led to her arrest, being initially sent to Auschwitz as a political prisoner and from there on to Birkenau. Her death was by cyanide poisoning.

The whole research process was evocative and filled with an intense mix of emotions. In my heart I felt that I was, or had been, Lisette. Would it be worth making extensive enquiries from authorities in Belgium? Did she have any family members still remaining that could be contacted? If so, would it even be possible to locate them and how would my story be received? Countless questions whirled through my head for weeks. There were two factors that I felt lent credibility to the possibility that I'd been Lisette in another lifetime. The first had been the physical manifestation of a cellular memory. I didn't imagine the bloodied mouth and blisters or the words that I'd heard clearly just before awakening some years earlier. The second factor was that at different times I was able to explain things about life and conditions during World War II that consciously I'd had no knowledge of. The frisson of energy that would move along my body often was my intuitive way of saying "Yes, that's correct," whenever yet another piece of the puzzle was uncovered or solved.

During the time of undertaking this research there were many memories that surfaced, some extremely uncomfortable and painful. The research, however, finally put to complete rest the nightmare episodes, fascination or obsession with all things relating to the Resistance and the subconscious fears of authority figures. The possibility of exploring this other lifetime further crossed my mind for some time, yet eventually I felt guided to let it be.

∞∞∞∞

The concept of reincarnation is written about extensively in Eastern philosophies and faiths. If this were truly to be the case then the concept of past lives also has to have merit. I wonder if in exploring the life of

Lisette and its possible connection to my current life I was researching a past life or maybe something else. Like many individuals espousing spiritual beliefs, rather than holding a religious faith, I'd been lured into believing that the cycle of reincarnation and past lives was a definite reality. For some years I happily talked about past lives as though they actually existed and were factual.

Among the many unexplainable experiences over the years I'd actually had a zoned-out meditative interlude where I'd been shown my Akashic Records. These are the record of all lifetimes lived, and mine passed by in a rapid whirl. I'd had other indications of having lived in other times, some of which held a lot of information. All these experiences supported my belief in the reality of reincarnation and past lives. My experiences with the bloodied mouth and blisters cemented those beliefs fully. When channelling the energy of Edgar Cayce he even made several statements supporting the existence of the reincarnation cycle. So, surely there had to be some substance or truth to the existence of a reincarnation cycle and past lives. Or maybe was it something else?

In spiritual teachings a great deal has been made around the importance of living in the moment. This concept has become somewhat of a commonly accepted belief within society in general. But what does it really mean? My teachers from the Arcturus Community focused on my learning, understanding and using energy in all aspects of daily life. Their teaching was pivotal to my later research, which included attempts to make sense of quantum physics and quantum consciousness. This whole field of science is too complex for a non-scientific mind such as mine. Regardless, I was able to make simplistic sense of some of the basics and in doing so there was a radical shift in both thinking and understanding.

The understanding of what is meant by the statement that all times exists in the Now moment took on new meaning. If, according to the quantum sciences, there is only the Now moment then there is no such thing as a past or a future. This logically means that all time must exist simultaneously. What is perceived as being in the past is happening now, just as the future is already happening. That awareness hit me like a sledge hammer as it came into consciousness. The awareness that only the present Now moment exists felt overwhelming and took a long time to grapple with. It was difficult to reconcile this awareness with all the previous understanding and knowledge acquired. With that awareness came a massive re-think around beliefs and truth. Understanding of the process came gradually, and to this day I'm still not sure if the way I view it is scientifically correct. Most likely it isn't but at this stage it's the most plausible way of explaining and understanding the nature of my reality.

Nowadays I see that all life times are lived simultaneously and that what happens in any one lifetime can, and does impact all other lifetimes. This is why I experienced the bloodied mouth and blisters. It also explained all the stomach pains throughout most of my life. There was some kind of energy 'bleeding' occurring between the lifetimes. While I have not shared the countless different energy memories from other lifetimes that have surfaced in my body there's no doubt that they are real and relate to experiences that have not occurred in this current lifetime.

I no longer talk about reincarnation as if it actually exists and when asked about past lives I respond with the words 'other lifetimes'. My current understanding of the teachings about the reincarnation cycle is that it's another mechanism for maintaining control over the general population. This understanding may change in time depending on possible new revelations; learning is always an ongoing process. The Buddhist philosophy teaches that in order to access Nirvana then good deeds are needed lifetime after lifetime until such time that Enlightenment occurs. At the risk of offending religions and other faiths' doctrines and practices it seems that control is exerted via any teachings that say we aren't good enough, that atonement is necessary and that ultimately a power outside the individual is the arbiter of whatever fate awaits the individual. My new understanding is that each soul is sovereign and is in charge of its divine destiny. The wisdom and awareness lies fully within each individual, along with responsibility for all choices made.

"The only limit to your impact is your imagination and commitment."

Anthony Robbins

CHAPTER 20

Luckily the ugly mouth syndrome (bloodied and blistered) lasted only a few days, and there was no sign of scarring. What was especially notable about the experience was the complete lack of pain. If the blisters had actually been a physical condition there is no doubt my mouth would have been tender and aching. At that time all I could hope for was that my body would not be subjected to any other energy memories manifesting into physical symptoms in the future. At the same time I was in awe of the physical body's capabilities while wondering just how many diagnosed modern illness conditions were actually no more than cellular or energy memories manifesting for a brief period of time.

Once this little episode though significant in many ways was over, the energy of Edgar once again began to dominate my life. It was unavoidable. His ever present energy within my body could not be ignored and gradually his periods of silence lessened. Many of my initial reservations about this whole experiment, which was how I'd initially thought of it, faded due to the highly respectful manner he carried at all times. The greatest volume of information shared about the commingling process occurred at night where Edgar would share what was happening and why, thereby helping both acceptance and understanding enormously.

Nearly eighteen months after the acupuncture session where Edgar's energy had whooshed into my solar plexus our public work together commenced. I was extremely nervous about appearing publicly and channelling his energy. I had moved to the North East where the life work of Edgar Cayce was highly respected and well known by many individuals. In fact, I'd go so far as to say that my knowledge of his life work was negligible. In accepting this role as a channel I actually felt as though I was being thrown to the lions; that there possibly might be scorn, derision and scepticism from attendees at channelling events.

The first public channelling session was the toughest. There was a small group of attendees and I was extremely nervous, mentally questioning my ability to provide a solid channelling of relevant information. Edgar was keen and started almost immediately once I relaxed into the trance state. When in the channelling trance I heard the individual words but was unable to make sense of coherence or fluency. Afterwards I was completely drained and it took nearly an hour to come back to full physical awareness before I was able to undertake the long drive home. This recovery experience was completely unlike any I'd had previously and was cause for concern. I had channelled light beings for about ten years by then and usually only felt a tad discombobulated afterwards, mildly tired but it wouldn't normally take long to feel renewed. Sometimes I found that undertaking light and restful activities for about half a day afterwards was sufficient restorative.

My diet continued to be healthy, organic, vegetarian and consisted mainly of raw foods. After that first public channelling I was completely exhausted for about a week. Muscle testing indicated that my body had become depleted in all vitamins, minerals and trace elements, something that had never occurred before. The vibration, or frequency of Edgar when channelling was obviously extremely high in comparison with my personal vibration. All the many energy downloads over the years, healthy and clean living practices, meditation and more had definitely shifted my personal vibration, but not enough! Edgar's energy when fully expanded within and beyond me was an exceptionally high frequency. The other factor that impacted my physical body was the length of the channelling period. It became commonplace for the channelling sessions to last between sixty and seventy-five minutes. This was far longer than any previous channelling undertaken.

The first three months of channelling were intense and involved a great deal of learning and adjustment in my life. I had been fortunate to have the support of a few close friends who understood channelling and its impact on the human body. One friend in particular mentioned that one hour of trance channelling was equivalent to doing about ten hours of intense physical activity. My acupuncturist friend, Gabi, was a mine of information in regards to Edgar's habits when he was alive. Apparently he preferred protein rich food when he was doing his trance readings. As a long-term vegetarian the thought of eating hamburgers was repugnant. Instead I ate vegetarian burgers and other protein rich plant based foods, which meant that the amount of protein in my diet increased dramatically.

I started eating peanuts, a favourite of Edgar's when he was alive I sensed but it was never one of mine. Protein foods were on the menu three times daily. High quality supplements were incorporated. As my body gradually adjusted to the energy of Edgar Cayce there were further changes to what I perceived to be an already healthy diet. I learned that a body vibrating at a higher frequency needed foods of a high frequency, mainly organic live foods. This meant that eating fast foods and highly processed, nutrient deficient foods was completely out of the question.

It wasn't long before other changes were evident. Unanticipated desires or cravings popped up strongly. The craving for fresh strawberries with cream surfaced one day. This wasn't a dish on my regular menu due to a lifelong lactose intolerance. However the craving was intense and required a modicum of creativity. Instead of rich cream I made cashew cream which was liberally slathered over recently purchased strawberries. The one craving that would not be satisfied was the strong desire for coffee. Years earlier the Arcturians had asked that I refrain from alcohol and coffee consumption due to the fact that they both have a deleterious impact on the human energy field. I was already struggling to hold a sufficiently high frequency in order to be a clear channel for Edgar's energy so compromising my vibration for one of his coffee cravings was definitely not going to happen.

Prior to the commingling of Edgar's energy with mine I had been a raw foodist for about three years. My body felt exceptionally healthy and strong, and had limitless energy for each day's activities. Once his energy became more settled within my body it became increasingly difficult to maintain the raw food lifestyle, due largely to the food cravings that surfaced continually. Another change that rapidly became obvious was a decreased desire to undertake regular intense exercise. Instead a daily walk ended up being the extent of any exercise routine while gym membership became obsolete. Increased sensitivity also occurred, meaning that psychic abilities and understanding expanded rapidly. Edgar also introduced me to the language that was common during his time on the planet and often I heard (in my head) and then used words I had no previous knowledge or understanding about. Many times a mad scramble to the dictionary or computer ensued to find the particular word and its meaning. His word usage was always correct and fully accurate in context.

Merging with the energy of Edgar Cayce helped shift erroneous thinking further. Negative thoughts and emotional patterns underwent a gradual shift; these are toxic and damaging to the higher frequencies. Gradually feelings of gratitude and appreciation were amplified, resulting in a more harmonious inner reality. Often, when working with clients, I quoted the Bible. The quotations were always apt and relevant to the individual's situation. The Bible quotations came straight from Edgar as I'd parted ways with organized religion and its teachings when younger. Edgar Cayce, however, when alive read the whole Bible once a year for every year of his life. In a private conversation he shared that in his last lifetime he had chosen to fully immerse himself in Christianity and its teachings. Ironically when he was alive he also had psychic and paranormal experiences. To this day I have no idea how that complemented or possibly was detrimental to the teachings of his religion.

My understanding is that the commingling of two soul energies is not a common occurrence. There have been reports of walk-ins, where one soul takes over as another leaves the body. Commingling is vastly different. I took on aspects of his character. My sense of self expanded; increased self-confidence also resulted in addition to greater comfort in coping with public exposure. It rapidly became obvious that in order for this commingling to be successful I needed to lift my game and that required considerable effort, time and energy.

∞∞∞∞∞

Some years earlier Carol had told me forthrightly that I was both a channel and an alien. I certainly didn't feel like an alien but realistically I had no idea exactly how an alien should feel. The sense of being different and not fitting in still surfaced with regular monotony. The difference by this time was that I was more accepting of it and had come to terms with the fact that my life would never again resemble the kind of life experienced by many other people. Even though I felt accepted and part of a larger group of metaphysical and spiritual people I realized that some of the incidents that occurred were well outside the realms of normal, even within this non-normal grouping.

The commingling of energies with Edgar Cayce was unique and it was beyond my comprehension that it could even happen. Once in conversation with a friend who also channelled I asked, "Why me?"

"Why not you," was her response as she then pointed out the extent of inner work, emotional healing and more that I'd undertaken over the years.

She was correct. For some inexplicable reason something from deep within had continually impelled me to be as clean as possible on the physical, mental, emotional and spiritual levels. Practitioners of Feng Shui focus on clearing the clutter in their home and/or working spaces in order to ensure the free and effortless flow of energies. In much the same way I had focussed on clearing the clutter within. When I commenced this purging process I hadn't realized just how much there was to clear. Nevertheless, my ego mind had felt satisfied, even complacent, with its achievements prior to commingling with the energy of Edgar Cayce. That bubble of self-satisfaction was quickly burst as it rapidly became apparent that another steep learning curve loomed.

Channelling regularly to groups for long periods was an entirely new and different experience. Each session involved providing an introduction, or explanation of the processes I'd undergone and an explanation of the channelling process. After the channelling there were questions and discussion. At all times I was under public scrutiny, though at the time that fact wasn't even on my radar. Instead, I felt it important to fulfil the arrangement or agreement that Edgar and I shared.

At times I was challenged by members of the audience. This was due to the fact that Edgar would be open to respond to questions once the main part of the channelling had been completed. Not everyone appreciated or accepted what was said. Many individuals sought medical insight into illness conditions experienced and Edgar made it abundantly clear that it was not his purpose to provide that. His intention with the commingling was to provide information about the transformative changes that were occurring upon the planet, along with the ramifications of those changes.

During each channelling session I heard the words but wasn't able to focus on them or fit them into a semblance of cohesiveness. The words were spoken in a structured manner, with hesitations and repetitions. It was not until later, in the privacy of my home that I was able to hear the recorded channelling and then transcribe it. There were times when I personally felt responsible for what had been channelled in a session and would bear the brunt of individual complaints and frustrations. What made this worse was the fact that I personally had absolutely no idea of what had been said or the context in which it had been expressed. I rapidly learned the art of walking a fine line of diplomacy and tact as a result.

With regular speech words are expressed and come from both conscious and sub-conscious mind. Trance channelling is different. Information transmitted bypasses the conscious, subconscious and super-conscious minds of the channel. Initially I would go into a relaxed state, which with practice was rapidly followed by a meditative trance state. An appropriate analogy to explain this is to refer to meditation. Initially when relaxing into meditation the alpha state is achieved, this is where the brainwaves slow down. After a while there may be a shift into the deeper theta state. In some instances the advanced meditator may experience the delta state, which is what the brainwaves show when in deep dreamless sleep.

My experience with trance channelling involved being somewhere between the theta and delta states in most instances. There are no thoughts, emotions or images present. It is a state of complete emptiness where there is little or no awareness of what occurs in the surroundings. It is an extremely comfortable and relaxing state. Every bodily function feels as though it has either ceased or is in a state of suspension, and that surely would have to be highly beneficial to health in so many ways. There are no earthly cares, there is no stress.

When channelling Edgar it didn't take long to enter into a relaxed state before feeling his energy expanding within and then beyond my physical body. As the expansion occurred the 'me' consciousness slipped away. After that there was only the deep empty space. Initially when this occurred I became very aware of another personality emerging and becoming dominant. This was not a schizophrenic occurrence, as there would be no voice speaking inside my head. Instead all I felt was expanded energy and emptiness, which was really a soothing and deep silence. After that, awareness of deep breathing occurred. Then the action began. A voice, bearing no resemblance to mine, would begin speaking and would continue speaking for as long as was necessary. Prior to each channelling I had absolutely no idea of topic content or its relevance to the audience.

Edgar always seemed to know exactly what was relevant and appropriate for each audience. Many times he displayed humour, hints of frustration and even impatience on the odd occasion. Overall the feedback received in the two years in which I channelled his words to audiences indicated that his language, tone, repetition and verbal idiosyncrasies were very similar to the transcriptions that had been undertaken of over fourteen thousand trance readings he had given when alive. In addition, often I was told by attendees at the sessions that transfiguration of my features occurred when channelling. This means that my facial features changed during the channelling and many individuals actually saw the face of Edgar Cayce super imposed over my features.

∞∞∞∞

One of the reasons I valued the channelling was that it provided an opportunity for listeners to reflect on their life purpose, on the meaning of existence and offered insight as to the nature of their core essence or being. Channelling provided insight that the external reality is merely a temporary state, and that everything needed comes from within.

Edgar taught the importance of always checking within for all answers. The human body really is the barometer of the soul. It continually emits subtle, and at times not so subtle signals regarding its response to internal and external stimuli. Unfortunately this valuable tool for gauging what is in alignment with needs and wellbeing is not greatly understood or valued in our western culture.

A great deal of the channelling focused on the importance of transforming from within. An introduction to one of his messages began with these words.

"Right now my energy is here with this one (me) at all times but I am also elsewhere. This is something you may have difficulty grappling with.

Your mind may feel as though this cannot be possible, and then you may say, "Well, if it's possible how can this take place?" The reason you may find it difficult to understand — and it's not for lack of trying, it's certainly not for lack of intelligence — the reason you may have some difficulty in understanding this is that you are a product of your environment, just as I was many years ago when I was in body. You believe to be the truth all that you have learned over the years of this lifetime. Correct? That is the truth. As you grow and have experiences in this lifetime your learning expands, as do your understanding and comprehension. Yet, to some degree you are still limited by the belief systems that are predominant within the society in which you live.

It is safe to remain within the constraints of those belief systems. When you remain within those constraints you do not upset other people. You know you are normal and so your thoughts are then reflected in your words and actions, and are perfectly acceptable, not only to yourself but to everyone else. That is the way it works. It was certainly like that in my last lifetime, and yes during my last lifetime I endeavoured my hardest to be normal. I did not want to be different, for we all know what happens to those who are a little different, don't we? They are the oddities, they are the ones that society will turn its back on and will think of as having a nut or two loose. You know what I'm talking about. So within the constraints of society everyone keeps playing the same game and the game is to be like everybody else. In being like everybody else, what happens? You squash creativity and originality. You contain and constrain yourself and any likelihood that you may just have a glimmering of something that is so different and unique to offer — to offer to other people, to offer to society. But you squash that because it is important to be normal and accepted."

"Your chances of success in any undertaking can always be measured by your belief in yourself."

Robert Collier

CHAPTER 21

More than two frenetically busy years were spent channelling the energy of Edgar Cayce to groups of people in the North East of the States. The months passed by in a whirl. When not actively engaged in channelling, transcribing and client work there was little time to spare for social activities. During this time radio shows were also hosted. I had become married to my work. Or to express it more aptly, work had become my mistress! By the end of each day it was a relief to relax and to feel the demands of a hectic work schedule fade away, for a few hours at least there was blissful relaxation. It did not occur to question the lack of balance in my life due to the fact that I thoroughly enjoyed my work. "Do what you love and love what you do," would have been my mantra at that stage. Work did not feel like work, it was passion; it provided satisfaction and enjoyment; and on a subtle level it felt like it was meant to be what it was. One distinct benefit was that I met and interacted with countless interesting, intelligent and beautiful people. The interactions and friendships that formed enriched life beyond measure.

The energy of Edgar petered out, in much the same way that my contact with the Arcturians had slowly faded. It was a natural progression and was rapidly becoming a familiar pattern in my life. However, despite the slow and steady disappearance of Edgar from everyday interactions my connection with him had not completely finished. By this stage I possessed a nice folder of channelling transcriptions and they were not meant to be stored in the back of a filing cabinet. I seriously considered leaving them untouched, knowing full well that by revisiting them the next phase of intense work would once again commence.

Regardless of my initial hesitancy time was then devoted to reading the channelling transcripts once again, several times over, with a view to creating a lasting memory of the shared time and experiences. Inevitably this led to the writing and publishing of another book. The exhausting work entailed in writing, publishing and marketing another book seemed never-ending. While writing is a solitary occupation the same cannot be said for the process of getting the written work out to the wider public. Once embarked upon there is little personal time left due to the constant communication required with the countless other people involved in getting a book into production and circulation. This time, however, the book marketing made greater use of the internet, online mailing lists and other electronic marketing tools. This necessitated a lot of new learning curves being undertaken. Baptism by fire would be one way of describing the process.

Book events locally along with a modified book tour were planned and organized. This time the book tour would be undertaken single handed. I would be unaccompanied, a fact I was deeply grateful for. Thankfully the travel was not extensive due to the largely successful online marketing and sales. The book tour included travel down to Washington DC and surrounding areas. Intuitively I had awareness that energy work would be undertaken on the earth and in specified areas while I was travelling. In particular, a great deal of attention needed to be paid to clearing the heavy, dark energies from the Pentagon. Instinctively I knew that this was a job too big for one person. My earlier experiences with clearing and dealing with dark, negative energies and forces would be insufficient for the task that lay ahead. There are times when a team effort is more likely to produce desired results.

It was definitely time to marshal the troops. Bulk emails were sent out to those on my mailing lists where I outlined what was needed and when. By asking for healing and light to be focused on the Pentagon for a period of several days I was hoping that the combined energies and intentions of many people would make a dent in the armoury of darkness within that particular institution.

When looking into the Pentagon clairvoyantly it was difficult to discern anything. The darkness was deep, like a solid mass of gooey black tar. On the journey towards Virginia there were numerous traffic challenges, the first and only ones on the whole trip. It felt as though there was an energetic blockage created to prevent my travels into the vicinity of the Pentagon. This resulted in another confrontation with the dark energies that were impeding my entry into the area. I had absolutely no interest in getting up close and personal to the Pentagon;

it was more important to be within the surrounding area. An intense and massive infusion of light energy was directed at the Pentagon for several days, with many individuals sharing the load. Unfortunately the result was not as anticipated. Numerous times I psychically scanned the building looking for some indication that there had been a measure of success. There appeared to be none. All those high hopes were savagely dashed. I wondered at my foolishness at even contemplating such an undertaking. The utter futility of it felt intense. In particular, this was not an outcome I was keen to share with those lovely souls who had responded to my request and had sent light and healing to the Pentagon and its vicinity.

Later on I had the clear awareness that despite appearances there had been a slight lessening of the dark energies. This obviously was one light versus dark battle that was too difficult and one that would not necessarily achieve my preferred outcome in a short period of time. It also indicated the extent of darkness and even evil that had penetrated and taken control. In the channelling sessions Edgar had indicated that there was a process of transformation occurring worldwide, and that this transformation basically involved a shift in consciousness. Being somewhat judgmental of what I was observing and sensing I could only assume that the vestiges of government and military would be among the last to shift in consciousness.

The power of group prayer or meditation has been shown to be successful in numerous instances. I'd previously read quite a bit about the ability of human intention to create positive change and healing, which was the reason behind sending out requests for support with this project. The power of many has the potential to change the world, especially when that intention is sent jointly and with the vibration of harmlessness and love being placed. As an empath and intuitive I'd become accustomed to feeling the vibe of a place and had become adept at avoiding locations that didn't resonate. Clairvoyantly I'd also seen the energies within and around many institutions and organizations. The Pentagon was, without doubt, the darkest of dark places that I'd ever encountered.

It had never been my intention to impose my beliefs or intentions on anyone else. It was not appropriate that I should determine what was right or wrong about a situation. Consciously I subscribe to the concept of freewill and acknowledge that all souls have choice as to actions and decisions. The decision to create a wave of healing and light energy to be sent by as many individuals as possible was not made by me. This was, yet again, another of those situations where the guidance from non-physical beings was strong and could not be ignored. One of my missions, or jobs as it might be called, in this lifetime was to connect with Mother Earth and to send healing when and where it's needed. The Pentagon, its influence and mission, has resulted in a great deal of damage to our precious planet. It's this fact, I believed at the time that resulted in a massive influx of light and healing energy being sent to that particular institution. Despite my initial disappointment at perceived lack of success there were moments of satisfaction due to the fact that the set intention had been carried out. It was not in my psyche to take failure, or anything for that matter too personally.

Life continued on as per usual. The workaholic treadmill kept whirring away. With the book tour completed and the energy of Edgar rapidly fading I was, once again, feeling that lack of guidance. I'd become used to hearing his wisdom and gentle exhortations and missed them as their frequency dwindled. It had become evident that a pattern of guidance had been established. Each individual spirit guide or community of guides would ensure an upgrade in my learning and understanding. Once their particular task had been completed they would gently fade away and I would feel bereft for a short while until the next phase of learning and growth commenced.

Each time a learning phase ended it actually felt like a significant and heartfelt loss, in much the same way as losing a loved one or having a friendship end. The loss was always incredibly tangible and real. This did not mean that the guidance was no longer there. It always was, just not as intense and obvious. Words of wisdom and support would always be whispered in my ear when needed. During these lulls my responsibility was to put into further practice all the learning that had been undertaken. This was done when working with clients, teaching classes and at other incidental times.

Not long after having my relationship with Edgar severed an unusual and unexpected event occurred. My client work involved working at different clinics and healing centres, which meant that often my day's schedule was filled with client appointments. On this particular day I headed out to a clinic about an hour's drive from home. About five minutes into the drive I began to feel extremely edgy. The desire to turn around increased and became intense. A mental checklist was undertaken. Had I left the stove on? Had the heater been switched off? Had I forgotten to lock the door?

My memory indicated that none of these were the reason for the discomfort and disquiet so I continued down the road a bit further. Instead of easing the urge to return home increased to an almost panicked state. I pulled off to the side of the road, quickly took out my phone and called the clinic.

"Something's come up and I have to turn around and check on some things at home. Would you mind calling the clients on today's appointment list and see if they will be okay with coming in thirty minutes later than their scheduled time?"

"What's happened? Are you okay?"

"I honestly don't know what's going on. It would be easy to say that I might have left something switched on at home but I don't think that's the case. Every instinct in my body is screaming out to turn around. I have to do this but I also know that I'll be there about thirty minutes later than the scheduled starting time."

"Okay, that's not a problem. You know what you need to do, even if you don't know why. If there are any other changes needed call back. We'll reschedule everything in the meantime."

With that organized it was with a huge sigh of relief I turned the car around and headed home. Once inside I double checked everything. There was nothing out of the ordinary. This meant I needed to dig deep psychically to see exactly what had prompted the strong inner urging and why.

More than fifteen years earlier I'd experienced a similar sensation. It was a gut wrenching intuitive knowing that something wasn't right. At that time while backpacking throughout the Mediterranean I had boarded a train for the overnight trip from Nice, France to Venice, Italy and had been excited about visiting this city that I'd read and heard so much about. However, almost immediately upon pulling out of the train station symptoms of unease surfaced. Fellow passengers were chatty and we shared stories about travel disasters and victories with a camaraderie that's reserved for backpacker tourists. It was impossible to ignore the feeling of unease despite the interesting stories and entertaining company. As the train continued its way towards Venice that feeling of dread increased. It reached an overwhelming and frightful ferocity. There was absolutely no way of curbing or controlling it, or explaining it away rationally. Upon arrival at Venice train station I hopped out, made a frantic beeline for the ticketing office, purchased a ticket for Florence and within ten minutes was on my way. As the train travelled away from Venice the tension in my body gradually abated. I eventually fell into a state of relaxed anticipation about the next city to be explored. There was never any insight or indication as to the reason for my body's reactive fear about visiting Venice. I merely trusted my gut instinct.

Now I was in New York, back in my secure home and wondering what the heck had happened. Why did that similar feeling erupt so suddenly and strongly? Was I being warned about something? I went into a light meditative state and asked, "What was that sense of sheer panic about? Why did it happen?"

Almost immediately a whole scenario unfolded in my mind's eye. It came into awareness in a nanosecond. A slew of information was presented as an intuitive knowing. If I had continued my journey at that time my car would have been involved in an accident. There would have been a head on collision due to the driver of the other vehicle being temporarily distracted, most likely by a phone call or message. The resultant outcome would have been a fatality – mine.

The information continued that I had completed all the tasks I'd set for this lifetime. My "To Do" list had been fulfilled and this would have been a chance to depart the physical body. The strong sense of unease was to alert me to the fact that an opportunity was being created for me to go home, back to the stars and constellations, if that were what I wished. Many years earlier I might have been excited about this opportunity, but not now. I certainly didn't wish to go home and knew if I didn't make my intention clear then another similar opportunity for this to happen would be presented in the near future.

With no real forethought about presentation I expressed my intention clearly and loudly, "I have no desire to leave this body. I'm not ready. There are still a lot of things I would like to see, do and experience in this lifetime. I don't know what needs to be done to ensure that my life continues for many, many years but I trust that it can and will be arranged. So be it."

With that intention clearly placed I phoned the clinic, told them I was on my way and arrived there thirty minutes later than originally scheduled to start the day's work. The whole experience had seemed surreal and later on when I recounted it to one of the staff at the clinic she totally accepted the reality of what had happened. What I hadn't anticipated was the follow on from this incident. Overnight life changed significantly. It took some time to figure out exactly what had happened and why.

The next few weeks were probably among the most stressful in a long while. My *modus operandi* for many years had been clearly defined and evident. I had drive, inspiration, determination and limitless energy. I was a master of manifestation. I made things happen. Each day's schedule was clearly mapped out mentally in advance. Intuitively I sensed that on a subtle level I had been following, or adhering to, a set internal program. This program, while invisible and unavailable to my consciousness was nevertheless the force that guided whatever transpired in my life. There was always something that could be, and needed to be undertaken and completed. Being at a loss as to direction and lacking drive to create and achieve was anathema and foreign in every respect. But that is what happened. Suddenly there was a massive chasm opening up right in front of me. Drive and motivation disappeared faster than a river in times of drought. There was no internal mechanism triggering enthusiasm. The spark had been extinguished. Mentally and emotionally this was nothing short of a major disaster. All that I had worked towards and created lay meaningless in a crumpled heap.

Countless self-examinations ensued. What had I overlooked? What needed to be done? Was this a temporary aberration or something more significant? No matter which way I approached this situation I found myself at a dead end. Idleness and slothfulness had never been part of my life, yet it felt as though I was rapidly sliding into a state of dissipation and disintegration. Nothing I did could stop this downward spiral. I suspected that the first indications of depression were setting in. There was no spark, no interest in anything. Zilch. Nada. Zero. Aimlessness and futility were rapidly becoming my new best buddies. And the worst part was that I felt powerless to stop this from happening.

Then, as if by magic, there began a subtle and steady turnaround. Motivation to create slowly began to re-surface. Imagination once again made intermittent appearances. Little by little I began to see an emerging picture. Change was a-coming. Not immediately but it was beginning. The vibes for a shift were emerging. In the meantime I was to continue on as previously seeing clients, teaching, mentoring or whatever else was needed. When the time was right I would be leaving New York. My inner knowing would guide me. Somehow I intuitively sensed that another, and new, chapter in my life had been planned and was about to be implemented. My command that I be given many more years of life had been heard and heeded.

"My darling girl, when are the young going to realize that being "normal" is not necessarily a virtue? It sometimes rather denotes a lack of courage."

Aunt Frances

CHAPTER 22

Often it felt both a blessing and a curse to be able to access information from the non-physical beings that had been my companions for practically all my life. I had come to value and rely upon their input and information. This did not necessarily mean I always obliged their guidance. Rebellion had been instilled into my being from a very early age. I'd learned to play the game, to appease the adults who controlled the ins and outs of my life. Despite this there were many indications of both defiance and rebellion being prevalent within my psyche from the very beginning.

I was determined to march to the beat of my own drum and every little act of rebellion spelt success in maintaining an ability to make decisions for myself. Sadly all too often I appeared to be conforming to others' wishes and expectations when in reality I railed against doing so. It would result in small, subtle acts of defiance that proved to ego that I exerted some measure of control over my own life, even when often it felt otherwise. If and when mistakes happened, as they often did, I rapidly viewed them both as a personal failure and as an opportunity for additional learning. For some inexplicable reason it was not in my nature to dwell too long on what might have been or what might happen in the future.

In metaphysical and spiritual teachings the word 'lessons' is referred to frequently. Every major challenge is often viewed as a lesson to be learned and mastered. Countless times clients have asked, "What is the lesson for me around this issue or situation?" When the energy of Edgar was present he indicated that life was not about having lessons to learn. He then shared that the word 'lesson' has strong connotations of either failure or success. Life is not meant to be about undergoing a series of failures or successes. Failure has its own dismal vibe, often resulting in feelings of inadequacy and creating inner stress. Success may result in initial feelings of euphoria but is often stressful due to the need to maintain that state by constantly striving to succeed.

Instead, Edgar indicated that life is simply about having experiences. These experiences result in increased awareness and understanding, which in turn results in further learning. The ultimate aim of all this is to assist and support the soul in its growth and evolvement journey. It's that simple. There are no lessons to be learned in life, only experiences for ongoing growth.

Luckily guidance from non-physical beings provided ample tuition and insights yet never told me exactly what I must do. Instead, they provided direction and encouragement. Choices were often presented. One time there was an option to purchase the house I was renting as the owner had decided to sell it. The asking price was higher than anticipated. The question asked was, "What is the best option? Buy this house or look for another house to purchase elsewhere and at a cheaper price?" Instead of a straight forward answer the pros and cons of each possibility were explained. I heard them clearly in my head. At the end of the explanation I heard the words, "It is a matter of choice. There is no right or wrong decision. It is merely a choice."

Once realization dawned that my command for many more years of life had been heard and heeded there was a subtle feeling of relief and also excitement. There would be many years of living still to be savoured and enjoyed. A feeling of wonderment and even euphoria emerged briefly. The logistics of the whole process was intriguing. What had been arranged? How had it been arranged? What did it mean? And, as per usual there was little or no communication from my spirit guides. I'd learned that when there is a need for communication from them it comes through. When I feel the need it doesn't necessarily happen. My desire to know more about the impending changes was non-stop. After being forced into idleness for several weeks it was not surprising that the desire for action was strong, a driving force that needed to be satisfied. My patience was low. Impatience to know more about the forthcoming changes simmered continually. The more I sought answers the greater the lack of communication.

Despite the knowing that I would be leaving New York there was no indication or signs as to when or where I would be heading. In fact, it was almost two years later that my future destination became apparent.

In the meantime I continued working in my practice and living life as usual. After the initial impatience I became more accepting of the *status quo*. The biggest difference was that I knew I was merely filling in time, going through the motions while waiting for the best timing for the unspecified changes still to occur. During this waiting time further incidents occurred that contributed to my understanding of energy, life, soul and more.

It was another busy afternoon at one of the clinics that I regularly worked out of. Clients had been booked in and as I was finishing the last appointment for the day I suddenly felt energy swirling all around me. It was exceptionally strong and it became difficult to remain standing upright without swaying. The energy not only spun around my body but also felt as though it was moving through every cell in my body. In particular, my head felt as though it was being rinsed clean by the energy moving in and out. In the middle of this happening I was still doing my best to be fully focused on my client and to complete the session to the best of my ability. He must have sensed something was different but didn't say anything. I apologized for not being myself; explained that something was happening energetically that was totally unfamiliar and out of my control. Any attempt to explain it was impossible so instead I was determined to minimize the impact of the energies and to end the appointment at the anticipated time and in a professional manner. Somehow I managed to carry it off, despite the fact that an inner turmoil was shaking my very foundations.

The sensation continued after my client departed. For some inexplicable reason I attempted to recall my mobile phone number. That was impossible. Then I racked my brain for my landline number and drew another blank. No matter what I attempted to recall I came up with emptiness. There was nothing. My memory was non-existent. With mounting panic I attempted to mentally recall my address. Again there was nothing. By this stage I was shaking and rapidly sinking into a frenzy of attempted memory recall. Every attempt turned up a blank response. Shaking badly I managed to pack up and tidy the consultation room before going outdoors. I needed to go home immediately and more than anything it was necessary to recall my phone numbers. If I could get them back then everything else would re-surface. Needless to say, my reasoning at that stage wasn't functioning too well and all

I could do was mentally attempt to bring up the digits of my phone numbers, again and again with no success.

Once inside my car with the engine started I began to worry that I might not be able to find my way home, especially given that I could not recall my address. The drive was the slowest and longest in living memory though in reality it took only about thirty minutes. Every intersection along the way was scrutinized several times as I attempted to figure out which way to drive. Somehow I eventually managed to pull into my driveway, get out of the car and through trial and error managed to find the key to open the door. The inside of my home looked both familiar and unfamiliar at the same time; a totally unnerving situation. I stumbled up the stairs to my office and started searching the drawers and files looking for pieces of paper that would reveal my phone numbers. With them in hand I then began reciting the numbers over and over again in an attempt to memorize and lock them permanently into some recall chamber in my brain or consciousness.

I had always found it easy to remember number sequences, which was probably why my focus had been on retrieving the phone numbers. This time, however, it wasn't easy to lock them back into consciousness, and I repeated them constantly. I spoke them aloud, wrote them on pieces of paper, tested my recall constantly, and this went on for what seemed like hours. My reasoning, however convoluted, was that if automatic recall of phone numbers occurred then everything else would be fine. It didn't work out that way. That night was difficult as I had to re-acquaint myself with my possessions and whatever else was taking up space in my home. By the time I went to bed a level of ease about the situation had developed, thanks to lots of steady, deep breathing. Whatever had transpired was energetic in nature. Exploration of the nature and cause of the experience had revealed that there was nothing physically the matter. My health was sound. Mental and emotional states were balanced, despite temporarily feeling otherwise.

The sensation of feeling unbalanced and discombobulated continued for several days. In time I recognized that a couple of things had occurred energetically, resulting in the frightening loss of memory. The first was actually an erasure of memory. As crazy as this sounds, and I definitely found it incomprehensible for a while, it actually ended up making a lot of sense. What is memory? Where is it stored? What is its purpose? These are not questions I'd normally ask, yet I know this experience produced significant shifts within.

After this incident there were definite and even massive gaps in my memory store. I found that reference to past incidents or situations no longer happened. In particular, minute details around the earlier years of my life became insignificant and remote, possibly because they had no basis in my current reality. The ability to live solely in the moment increased dramatically and was a most comfortable outcome.

The second aspect of the experience was that there was a shift in personal frequency. My vibration had shifted to a higher level, for want of a more suitable way of expressing it. Receiving this upgrade was the catalyst for the memory erasure, which was actually a momentous event and demonstrated, once more, the impact of energy upon the human body. My experiences over the years, I'd learned, were always the precursor to what other people would encounter in their particular life journey. Having undergone these weird and unusual experiences meant that I was able to understand and help others through similar processes.

Experiences such as the memory erasure were always disturbing and unsettling initially. I had no point of reference to be able to understand what had occurred. My non-physical friends were often tardy in providing information that would ease any discomfort or distress. Yet, ironically, the answers would always eventually trickle through into consciousness. Sometimes, the information would be provided via lucid dreams, other times a strong and concise knowing would envelop my being or often a mass of information would be encapsulated within a nanosecond of information download. This information would generally become available at times when my body and mind were at rest, often just before sleep, when driving my car or even when in the bathroom.

∞∞∞∞

From an early age I'd parted ways with the invisible being or entity called God. My faith in religions had been totally eroded. Even a short lived phase of interest in Buddhism had ended in disillusionment of the worst kind. Years had been spent looking for a spiritual teacher, and to no avail. I'd basically come to the conclusion that everything in creation is energy, including mere mortals and that there was, however, a creator source that exists within everything. This meant that the energy of the creator source exists within each human being and also within all that exists upon our precious planet and within the multiverses. This energy, in quantum science, has been shown to have both consciousness and intelligence. That being the case this consciousness rests within each person and does not originate from an outside source. My logic was simple. Handing over power and responsibility for my life didn't make sense as the creator source exists within.

I strongly believe in the concept of self-empowerment. Each individual is a sovereign being, a powerful soul. Once that awareness registers on a large scale there will be no authority to tell us how to behave, think and feel. The indoctrination by religions and different faiths has survived centuries. But just how much of what has been taught is truth? How much is used to enslave?

At an earlier stage in my communication with spirit guides I referred to them as being the "puppeteers" and myself as the "puppet". That comment was stated somewhat in jest yet I was immediately told, "We are all the same. We are equal. There is no control; there is only give and take." Many years later when channelling the energy of Edgar Cayce he stressed the importance of claiming "mastership". By this he meant that we are masters of our own destiny; that we are powerful autonomous beings and that everything we need rests within.

Instead, we have become inculcated into giving away our power and sovereignty again and again. Edgar stressed the importance of letting go of all beliefs, all understanding and all the former ways of functioning that had become habituated. In order to become one with this consciousness and intelligence a massive re-think is needed. Systems, beliefs and programming have led humanity into a state of separation, which in turn is further fuelled by the societal conditioning around the "Them" and "Us" mentality. Love is the one unifying factor. There can be no separation when there is only love. When there is only love there is no need for religions and faiths or systems of control as heart centred love will be the ultimate force that drives humanity. Ah, if only it were that simple!

One weekend morning, relaxing with a cup of herbal tea and sitting in my kitchen nook I was taken by surprise as a wave of energy emanated from the back of my head. Almost immediately I felt surrounded by another softer energy, supporting this wave that was being pulled out strongly. A suction force, never previously experienced, persisted. Ironically, despite the force of this energy movement pulling strongly my hair remained in place. By this stage I'd become accustomed to the bizarre and unusual energy shifts that occurred often and when least expected. This pulling sensation was sustained for quite some time. I remained seated and motionless. Curiosity was aroused. What the heck was this about? I'd already experienced the memory erasure, an experience I ended up feeling deeply grateful for. This energy withdrawal process felt different in many ways. It had strength and also depth. It also was focused fully around my head, especially the back and nowhere else.

Within seconds of mentally asking a slew of questions information roiled into awareness. All sub-conscious memory relating to religious beliefs, practices, indoctrination, and more were being suctioned out from the old instinctual, primitive brain located at the back of the head. As this was happening I clairvoyantly saw the memories of lifetimes of religious practice, indoctrination and torture being pulled out. Then came the awareness that on every level I was finally free from that control, however subtle and insidious it might seem. Several other moments of lucidity followed. Humanity has been immersed in superstitions, religious rites and beliefs through countless centuries. This has resulted in a form of enslavement and bondage that rests deeply within the human psyche. The benign aspects of this enslavement ensure its ongoing functioning. Souls that live many lifetimes absorb the doctrines of learning, accept them as being true and then perpetuate that in an ongoing manner. The enormity of this awareness remains to this day.

After this massive clearing there was no confusion or uncertainty. I felt clean inside and clear in thinking processes. Admittedly something felt different within for quite a while after this occurrence. Attempting to pinpoint the difference was futile initially but eventually I was able to explain it in one word – freedom! Entrenched beliefs and programs that impact thoughts and behaviours no longer impacted in any way. There was no longer any confusion about the nature of reality. It literally felt as though a dirty pair of spectacles had been removed and my vision was clear for the first time in my life.

Feelings of sub-conscious guilt no longer surfaced at odd and unexpected moments. It wasn't necessary to feel as though I should be playing the same game as everyone else. A stronger and clearer sense of self gradually emerged; it was a healthier and more balanced sense of self. Doubts and constant questioning seemed to disappear. Instead a sharper sense of action and purpose appeared. I also became comfortable with making mistakes, often enjoying them whereas previously unbidden feelings of inadequacy and shame would have surfaced. My connection with spirit guides strengthened and I became more comfortable talking about my experiences with individuals when previously I would have held back. The feeling of true freedom within is heady. It continually feeds my soul.

"Although I am a typical loner in my daily life, my awareness of belonging to the invisible community of those who strive for truth, beauty and justice has prevented me from feelings of isolation."

Albert Einstein

CHAPTER 23

Going through the motions of life without the feelings of heart or joy is debilitating. All excitement is sucked out, leaving no more than an empty husk. That is how I felt for a long period of time after the distressing energetic memory erasure occurred. That memory erasure, while upsetting, was actually a blessing in disguise. I had learned that hanging onto memories of things that had happened was another way of living in the past, of focusing energy onto things that were not taking place in the present moment.

An initial feeling of lightness after the eradication occurred lasted a short while only to be replaced by everyday drudgery. The routine of a life that once provided excitement and stimulation now felt dreary, repetitious and monotonous. These feelings, and perception, were fuelled by the knowledge that change was a-coming, but it just wasn't evident anywhere on the horizon. And there were no indications of this impending change in the near future.

Being somewhat prosaic I ended coming to terms with the situation. Determined to make the most of each day I eventually had no choice but to accept the lack of immediate change. This was an ideal opportunity to practice the art of learning patience and honing it to the highest degree. If I'd not had the awareness of impending change my moods and attitude might have been remarkably different. But, sometimes having intuitive knowing of things is a double edged sword. There is a build-up of excitement and when expectations are not met immediately then a letdown is often painful. Mental reminders went along these lines, "Universal Now time is different to our human linear time."

Often I moaned about the non-stop work that came my way; next I grumbled about the fact that life wasn't exciting or something else. There were times when I observed great things happening in other peoples' lives and while thrilled for their good fortune would lament about the routine stodginess of my existence. Occasionally I would mutter, "When is it going to be my turn?" Apparently my grumbling and muttering were observed and heard by my non-physical friends because one day when out walking I heard clearly, "Ultimately the giving and receiving must be equal."

Such a simple, yet profound statement was a powerful reminder of the power that exists within and is also encapsulated within everything. Complete understanding of this statement accompanied the words. The words did not mean that for every action there was an equal and opposite reaction, as had been taught in high school science class. The meaning instead was that the giving and the receiving would not necessarily equal out at the time but over the course of a lifetime, or over many lifetimes, there would be that balance between the two. Nor was the statement necessarily about material or tangible objects or events. Mistreatment of others is as much of a giving as is a spirit of generosity. Whatever is given out is eventually returned in kind. Karma in action.

The power of this statement was sufficient to shift my dissatisfaction into a focus of gratitude and appreciation, albeit slowly. An attitude adjustment had been sorely needed. Simply by shifting thoughts it was possible to change perspective, and from there an emotional charge of gratitude emerged and gradually strengthened. This shift did not mean that life suddenly became idyllic. Far from it. Instead, it became bearable and acceptable. There were, once again, occasional moments of joy and lightness. My heart felt less heavy. Once again I was reminded that when the time was right then the anticipated changes would happen. I stopped worrying about things over which I had absolutely no control. This all sounds easy, but it was actually a process of further inner growth and change over quite a lengthy period. If I had attempted to create changes in my impatience they would have been unsuccessful. I was reminded of a time, many years earlier, when I'd been down a similar road.

At that time I'd been determined to create a number of initiatives in my newly established self-employed business. These initiatives were to be built up following specific steps that I'd determined were essential to any later success. An upgraded business plan had been developed. A great deal of time and effort had been involved in research, planning and its execution. Unfortunately things didn't turn out as anticipated. My ability to control outcomes was dismal. My desire to follow my planning step by step in a consecutive and methodical manner would shape management and business success, or so I believed. Nevertheless, every innovative step implemented met with zero success. In fact, struggle and I became very good friends. Difficulties and challenges met every potential opportunity.

When I mentally asked, "Why?" I clairvoyantly saw a steering wheel with both hands on it. This indicated that I was hanging on too strongly. It was time to let go of control. I stopped micro-managing every step of the way and gradually learned to trust. Once I took one hand off the steering wheel it was amazing to see how effortless the flow became, with more successes than I'd ever anticipated. However, every time I attempted to take full charge and control of things there, once again, would be a constriction of flow.

Sometimes it's necessary to be reminded of earlier learning and to once again reflect and refine that earlier understanding into something more erudite. It was time to fully live within the flow of life, whatever that flow might be. And to let go of any preconceived ideas or aspirations. This did not mean that having dreams and hopes was a futile exercise. Instead, it meant allowing what was meant to be to unfold one step at a time; or even better, to visualize each step just before its unfolding and to then allow it to unfold. The power of imagination was not to be undermined or limited in any way. Living this way meant letting go of a desire for specific outcomes.

One thing became very apparent is that when living in the flow of life there's greater ease and rapidity of movement right at the moment it's most needed. There is less constriction and certainly fewer impediments to achieving desired outcomes. So, I continued living each day as it unfolded, with fewer expectations and aspirations. The feelings of gratitude increased, along with a subtle acceptance that the long desired changes would occur when the timing was perfect for their appearance.

Long before I even fully knew or understood the nature of the impending changes I began the process of de-cluttering my home. Clothes, possessions, books, knick-knacks and everything considered extraneous were culled with a ferocity that was unexpected. The public library system was the recipient of a loved and pristine book collection. Giving away books that had been amassed over a period of years was painful; it felt like giving away an aspect of my soul to an unknown future. Furniture that was not needed was either sold or given away. Personal possessions that would remain with me were gradually packed into postal boxes, future destination as yet unknown. A significant chapter of my life was rapidly coming to an end. Closing this door meant that another would soon be opening.

I seemed to know in advance exactly what needed to be done while not knowing the exact nature of what was to follow. This is an interesting aspect of having intuitive abilities. It felt as though, once again, there was already a pre-determined destiny or fate involved. The concept of freewill once again reared its head. To what extent was I, the conscious ego me, in charge of these changes? Or was there an inner will that was more all-knowing directing the changes? Logically these questions, while pertinent, were irrelevant to the situation. I just knew what to do in preparing for the move, one step at a time, long before the change actually occurred. This indicated that when it was time to move then the momentum would be rapid and everything would happen in a relatively short period of time and with a forceful flow.

The changes, when they came, were swift and flowed effortlessly. Clients had been informed. Clinics and healing centres had been notified. Goodbyes said, often over long lunches or meals. The whirl of activity was intense and filled with excitement and goodwill. On another level the inner voice felt a sense of disquiet about the impending changes. Moving back to Australia, after these many years living in the States, would involve starting anew. Worst of all I had no real idea about where I would live or what would be needed to re-start the life that had been left behind. I had no home to return to. Intuitively I knew that this would be a fresh start and that there would be no carry-over from the hectic and satisfying life I'd lived overseas for many years.

∞∞∞∞∞

Almost immediately I began to understand how refugees must feel upon finding themselves in an unfamiliar and foreign environment. Years earlier I'd created a life for myself in the States with relative ease and minimal bureaucratic red tape or protocols involved. I did not recognize the Australia I returned to; it had changed significantly in the years I'd been away. The bureaucratic rigmarole entailed in starting anew was surprising, especially given the fact that my details were still retained within government systems. I felt like a stranger in a strange land once again and often would shake my head in incomprehension at the way things had become so institutionalized and systematized in such a short period of time.

My skills, knowledge and experiences developed overseas had absolutely no validity in Australia. Recognition of prior learning, a concept that had been embraced by learning institutions years earlier, I was informed would entail too much time and work to determine. In other words, it would be necessary to retrain in order to be qualified. The rebel in me quickly decided to reject this option. Instead, other options would be explored.

Any determination to create a career quickly evaporated due to perceived blockages that appeared constantly. I was reminded of the astrologer's words all those years earlier. She'd commented that when the doors of opportunity closed before I was able to enter them it was the Universe's way of gently guiding me to where I was meant to be. If I wasn't meant to continue working as I'd been doing then I'd better figure out quickly just what was intended. Little did I realize that the next four years were meant to be 'time out'; a time for reflection, a time for re-connecting with the Earth, a time for solitude and spiritual growth. Instead of constantly keeping busy with doing things I was eased into an existence of being. The difference between doing and being is vast and afforded an invaluable opportunity for further personal growth and inner expansion. For the first time in many years I'd been given time out for a sabbatical; this was sorely needed and long overdue.

When I channelled the energy of Edgar Cayce he was insistent about the importance of being rather than doing. His explanation for being was very simple.

"What does it mean to be in a state of being? The easiest way to explain this is to say that when you are being, you are not doing. Being is a state of existence – and that requires conscious application. Being is an important state that can be incorporated into any and every daily routine. Within current lifestyle and functioning there is so much focus on constantly thinking and doing, which creates a lot of tension and stress within the body. Being is the exact opposite of doing and is a powerful way of reducing and relieving tension. When you take time to just be your body relaxes. Stress is

reduced and there is an inherent feeling of peace and wellness. Achieving a state of being is absolutely critical to wellbeing."

Many years earlier I'd read a book by Vicki Mackenzie, *Cave in the Snow*, about a Buddhist nun's retreat spent in a cave, away from civilization. She grew some vegetables and tended them. Local villagers also brought her food and would journey to the cave from time to time to ensure she was okay. The cave retreat was this nun's way of finding the stillness within and becoming one with creation. Many years earlier I'd also had the good fortune to hear her speak publicly about her challenges, experiences and learning during this time of isolation from the world.

Retreating from the distracting influences of the wider world was often the way that mystics and gurus gained deep and real understanding of the nature of reality. My four years' sabbatical was similar in intention but very different in practical reality. Instead of being actively involved in spiritual groups and activities I was now flung into a broader, more diverse society and was reminded starkly of other realities co-existing within the larger reality or world. Once again I became aware of my unusual perspectives on life. Instead of feeling out of place and different I rapidly realized that I'd fully embraced my uniqueness and no longer felt the need to hide or play the game in order to be accepted. In fact, that energy of being different, which once had felt extremely uncomfortable, no longer bothered me.

Opportunities to volunteer both time and skills to different organizations proved to be worthwhile. A great deal of the volunteer work was physical in nature, which was a bonus for physical health and wellbeing. Sharing of ideas and knowledge in fields other than esoteric studies was a novelty and also highly rewarding. Of particular importance were the opportunities to engage in working the land in a natural, sustainable way. Organic gardening, learning about permaculture and self-sustainable living provided a strong reconnection and bond with Mother Earth. Getting down and dirty with the earth was enriching and highly rewarding.

During the four years there were times I experienced periods of separation and felt extremely disconnected from spirit guides. I had been given time out for a sabbatical and it seemed as if my non-physical friends had stepped at least ten paces away and left me to my own devices most of the time. In fact, I'd been left to appreciate and enjoy the challenges of everyday life, and to apply all that I'd learned spiritually in a practical and relevant manner. Instead of relying on spirit guides for insight, guidance and support there was a gradual and incremental increase in self-reliance.

In the early stages of my spiritual journey I'd explored the concept of the existence of a higher self and had understood the existence of an energy link connected with the physical body. This energy could be called the soul, higher self, divine self, spirit or whatever other name was appropriate. Semantics are often used to describe a concept or issue in order to create common understanding. During meditations I'd seen this energy aspect of myself as being some distance away from my physical body and had invited it to meld, or merge, with my physical body. The higher self initially declined, indicated that my personal frequency needed to be raised before such a thing could happen. Thus began my serious journey as I worked at releasing old pain memories, beliefs and denser frequencies from my energy body. The day that I felt my higher self merge within was a day for great celebration. From that day onward the communication between us increased and gradually stabilized. I learned to fully trust whatever information was given, and came to see that my higher self was the conduit to universal consciousness.

Communication with higher self is vastly different to that shared with spirit guides, or non-physical beings. Higher self speaks simply, usually in mono-syllabic form. It provides warning when danger lurks. It guides simply in a straight forward manner when direction is needed. Higher self communicates clearly and in a consistent straightforward tone. Spirit guides, however, express themselves simply or can be loquacious, depending on what is needed. There are differences in tone and intonation depending on the energy of the spirit guide. Over time I learned the subtle differences. Nevertheless communication from either was always consistent, reliable and accurate.

During this time of enforced sabbatical and distancing from spirit guides I relied on both higher self and gut instinct to validate decisions that needed to be made. The days of using logic for decision making had long gone. Often my body's instinctual response provided the answers needed when decisions were required. More and more the inner knowing came to the fore, with sudden and inexplicable force.

One such knowing occurred after time spent, once again, reflecting on what I perceived to be my inability to remain in casual or long-term relationships. Basically my record for relationship longevity was pathetic and had been the cause of both shame and regret. This particular knowing, when it surfaced, was forceful and especially clear. At a soul, or higher self, level this was not meant to be my path in this lifetime. I came into this body to lead a spiritual gypsy lifestyle, unencumbered by the constraints of committed romantic relationships. It was especially important that I be free and unfettered in order to continue and complete my soul plans that had been put in place long before I incarnated.

While this deep knowing clarified and explained a lot I wasn't impressed that it had taken so long for the obvious to become fully apparent. The possibility that I was a very slow learner was a thought that was entertained for some time. A great deal of heartache and frustration could have been avoided had this clear and insightful knowing been evident decades earlier. Instead, I'd twisted myself inside out attempting to conform to societal norms, and had frequently believed that possibly something was inherently wrong with me. Why was it deemed necessary to live in committed relationships? Who or what had instigated this system as being the preferred and normal way of life? Obviously government and religious systems had colluded in creating this socially accepted institution, and not necessarily for the highest good of all people.

Again the awareness regarding the high level of indoctrination that had occurred within our co-created reality was immediate and intense. Just about every institution or system established within our culture did not support free will. Instead, controls existed on every level ensuring compliance and conformity from an unsuspecting and duped public. It never ceased to amaze me just how much lucidity and clarity surfaced every time there was yet another significant ah-ha moment. In those moments I was able to also extrapolate from my position, perspective and understanding to see what was happening on a larger scale.

There was no doubt about it. The price of non-conformity was high, but the personal price of conforming to societal norms was even higher.

"Your universe begins within you. Everything outside of your consciousness is an extension of you. That includes your guides, your teachers, your lessons, your world and your physical reality. You create your reality."

Unknown

CHAPTER 24

As with all sabbaticals there comes a time for an ending. Its purpose had been achieved, but it was only upon its completion that the full import of its purpose became evident. During the time spent getting down and dirty with the earth there were countless opportunities for connecting with individuals from a diverse mix of backgrounds and interest. Despite my personal quirkiness and interests it became apparent there was a great deal of commonality with others and the differences were often minimal.

It became obvious that I wasn't the only one holding feelings of being different. My desire to be true to myself was equally bestowed upon others who were also becoming aware of the deeper truths inherent in our true nature. The worldwide awakening in consciousness was becoming apparent. Almost everyone I connected with during this four year hiatus shared their story and their perceptions. My voluntary absence from the life I'd known for so long offered glimpses of hope for the future of humanity. This was a time of being humbled by the tenacity evidenced in others and their determination to make sense of a chaotic time in history, while simultaneously coming to terms with their personal shifts in understanding.

While my self-imposed sabbatical was more physical and my level of daily activity increased significantly there were also other changes occurring within. Often deep feelings of aloneness were all pervasive though loneliness was never a factor. My reflections went along the lines of, "Feeling alone is preferable to feeling lonely or feeling alone in a relationship." It is during times of solitude and introspection that often the greatest shifts in healing and understanding arise.

The utter futility of life often struck me once again. No longer seeking to work full time the future horizon had the potential to look gloomy and uninspiring. All that had been important when working with clients and continually striving to make a difference in the world disappeared and dissolved into nothingness. The treadmill of existence, the life path options and choices made at times seemed pointless in the long run. Achievements, successes and feelings of satisfaction ultimately would come to mean very little. They were history, part of my past but existed no more. Was life only about waking up each day, repeating the daily patterns and routines, going to bed and then repeating that routine day after day? In reality any minor excitements and changes in routine would effortlessly slide into memory before too long. Ultimately, what did life matter? What was the real purpose of existence in a human body? Why the hell was I here?

The answer was readily within the grasp of my consciousness. I kept sensing creativity or the ability to create as being essential to survival and even for the ability to thrive. But exactly what is creativity? Or maybe it was merely the ability to create rather than actually possessing strong creative abilities? When looked at that way I began to glimpse a sense or purpose for life. Creation, or creating, is what happens daily. Every thought, whether through imagination or conscious application contributes to the overall creation and manifestation of our co-created reality.

If the purpose of life is to create then the next question would be what needed to be created, or how to create purposefully? While pondering deeply upon the concept of creation as an active and conscious application I still was no closer to figuring out how it applied to my current mental and emotional state. My feelings of usefulness and purpose had dried up. I was feeling my age. The encroaching old age syndrome loomed and my value in the world was questioned extensively. No doubt about it, inspiration was sorely lacking. Yet, having experienced lulls in activity and creativeness previously I was aware that often the lull of nothingness precedes a period of intense activity.

Suddenly and unexpectedly, night after night I would awaken between two and four o'clock aware that a slew of words were running through my head. The words made perfect sense and they flowed rapidly. They were the words needed to write the next book. Both title and sub-title of the book were provided. It was time, once again, to figuratively chain myself to the computer and allow the mental flow of words to be translated into a tangible form. The emerging compulsion to write was overpowering and all consuming. Was this a download of information? Or was it an exposure to what had been sitting in the subconscious mind for a long period and now needed to be released? My creative urges were once again on fire and craving expression. The creative drought was over. Finally!

During the writing process new spirit guides made their presence felt. This new non-physical energy was strong, yet exceptionally gentle and powerful at the same time. It enveloped me often and all I felt was a high frequency of pure and divine love as further downloads of electrical currents would course through my body. The arrival of this community of non-physical beings indicated that once again it was time to re-commence the work I'd left behind four years earlier but in a new and as yet unfamiliar vein. Sabbatical was definitely over, retirement was no longer an option. Preparation for the next phase in life commenced.

∞∞∞∞

The pain in my mouth felt knife sharp and red hot at the same time. I wanted to curl up, scream out loud and blank out all the pain simultaneously. Breathing was short and laboured. Eyes watered in pain. It hurt to think or function. To make matters worse there was not one pain killer in my medicine cabinet. I didn't believe in them and for the life of me couldn't figure out why I'd ever come to that conclusion. For once the brave, stoic me was totally non-existent. Pain and I made lousy partners. Being an empath and highly sensitive increased the pain level many times over. Even the therapeutic grade essential oils applied frequently and liberally did nothing to alleviate the debilitating pain that lasted for the longest week of my life.

The fact that I wasn't able to identify exactly the origin of the pain made it all the more confusing and unnerving. It was located on mainly the left side of my mouth, in my jaw and gums and would also travel across to the right side. Both sides of the jaw felt as though they were glued shut. Eating food, especially chewing, amped up the pain level to an all-time excruciatingly high level.

The worst aspect of all was my inability to figure out what was happening and why. Many possible reasons and scenarios flitted across my mind. All were plausible and made sense, yet none fully felt right.

Mental dialogue was straight forward. "Is it in my best interest to go to a dentist?"

"No."

"Do I have an infection in my mouth?"

"No"

"Should I go to a doctor?"

"No."

"Is it a physical issue?"

"No."

"Is it energetic in origin?"

"Yes."

Through this familiar mental dialogue process I was able to determine that there was a major emotional component to the pain, which meant that pain medication wouldn't have made an iota of difference if I'd even had any in my bathroom cabinet. Mentally I commanded that any and all emotional pain and memories be cleared with love. A simple command, but it was effective because within twelve hours I felt extremely nauseous for about half a day. The feelings of nausea along with a complete lack of appetite always accompany the release of emotional issues. Over the course of the previous quarter of a century I'd learned this fact many times over. Yet, the overall pain level only reduced slightly. By this time I was fed up with only consuming smoothies and other liquids and despite every reasonable guess was still unable to actually fathom the underlying emotional reason for the pain.

Unexpectedly the phone rang. "How are you?" Isla asked. "Your name's been popping into mind so often these past few days so I thought I'd better call."

I began talking about the pain and my educated guesses as to its cause. Isla interrupted, "How's the book coming along?"

"It's nearly finished."

"The pain is emotional, and it's been suppressed since you were young. It goes all the way back to your mother, and she's the reason you were never allowed to speak up, that because of this you've kept your real self hidden from the world. Your mother's lack of support throughout life didn't help. Something happened and you weren't able to express yourself for a large part of your life. Your mother couldn't accept that you're different, that you didn't conform. The stress of holding back, of not speaking your truth is now finally releasing."

I felt a wave of goose bumps along my body, confirming the veracity of her words. Interestingly Isla had no previous knowledge of what she shared. I had not opened up about my earlier years, having adopted my mother's mantra that something in the past could not be changed so therefore there was no point in rehashing ancient history. Prior to this I'd already spent a great deal of time years ago doing forgiveness work and letting go of emotional wounds as they arose. I seriously thought that I was at peace with whatever had happened within our mother-daughter relationship, irrespective of its dysfunctionality. Obviously there was further work to do, as this manifestation of emotional pain into excruciating sensations in my mouth was of a high intensity. It definitely reminded me of the many times I'd had to zip my lips for fear of censure and disapproval.

The pattern for this had been repeated throughout my life, in both friendships and relationships. Maybe now the sub-conscious fear of speaking my truth, of being ridiculed and of being different could be put to rest once and for all.

After speaking with Isla for a bit longer I reflected on the dynamics of the whole experience and had another profound insight. Years ago I'd had the strong awareness that when I was still forming in the womb my mother had learned of my father's infidelity. As a result she did not wish to remain pregnant. Obviously no abortion resulted. The shock of discovering this infidelity had reverberated throughout my as yet unborn body, resulting in some form of energetic shattering deep within. The memory of not being wanted, of not being accepted just possibly might be the core issue, or a root cause of all that had prevented open and honest self-expression throughout my life. It might not even be in my true nature to be wary of sharing myself openly. It might in fact be a condition or issue of transgenerational patterning. In other words, most likely I had taken on my mother's pain and beliefs when in the womb and they had consequently become internalized into my psyche.

With this awareness and understanding a steady feeling of peace and acceptance seeped into my being. Along with this there was significant regret and sadness. Sadness due to the lifelong impact that carrying my mother's pain had created. Sadness that this left me in a vacuum. Having taking on my mother's emotional pain and integrated them into practically all aspects of my life I was then left with little or no real idea of who I was, or what I would become as a result of this massive energetic release.

I reflected deeply upon the 'sins of the fathers' (and mothers) that are carried through the generations. When and how would the pain of humanity be released and healed? The likelihood of world peace seemed impossible, given the long chain of transgenerational patterning throughout many cultures. Many years earlier, at a time when there were reports of further atrocities, carnage and senseless killing worldwide I had questioned the likelihood of there ever being peace in the world and heard, "How can there be world peace when there is no peace in the hearts of humanity?"

The Dalai Lama at one time expressed a similar insight, though it was worded differently. He said, "Peace in the world depends on peace within. If we have that we can approach problems in a spirit of compassion, dialogue and respect for the rights of others – always a better solution than resorting to use of weapons and force. External disarmament depends on inner disarmament."

I had actually felt a sense of calm and even a semblance of peace within for quite a number of years and now this inner disturbance had arisen unexpectedly. However, I finally figured that as I healed this generational pain the impact of that healing would energetically support future generations in my family. Being energetically connected to the matrix that weaves its way through all of creation meant that any individual inner work undertaken would have a far reaching effect, far further than could possibly be dreamed.

"Is this it?" I asked. "Is this the final piece of the puzzle? Will it now be possible to live fully in joy and peace? Or, is there still further inner work to be done?"

Even as I asked these questions I knew the answer. Life is a never ending journey. A journey back to the self. To come back to the self means eventually coming to an acceptance of all that has transpired, to find that sense of inner harmony and peace, and to live life filled with heart centred unconditional love. My new determination was to now find the best version of myself and to become that version. If there is one more final achievement to be created it's to eventually leave this temporary home, my body, in a state of acceptance, peace and hopefully even joy. To cross to the other side with gratitude and serenity in my heart would make everything that's ever happened truly worthwhile.